WALKING IN THE BERNESE OBERLAND – JUNGFRAU REGION

50 DAY WALKS IN GRINDELWALD, WENGEN, LAUTERBRUNNEN AND MURREN

By Jonathan and Lesley Williams

JUNIPER HOUSE, MURLEY MOSS,
OXENHOLME ROAD, KENDAL, CUMBRIA LA9 7RL
www.cicerone.co.uk

© Jonathan and Lesley Williams 2023
First edition 2023
ISBN: 978 1 78631 114 6

Printed in Singapore by KHL Printing on responsibly sourced paper
A catalogue record for this book is available from the British Library.
All photographs are by the author unless otherwise stated.

Route mapping by Lovell Johns www.lovelljohns.com
Contains OpenStreetMap.org data © OpenStreetMap
contributors, CC-BY-SA. NASA relief data courtesy of ESRI

*Our thanks to the late Kev Reynolds for all his encouragement
with this project, Caroline Holmes and Joe Williams for checking
the routes we couldn't, the support from all the tourist offices in
the Jungfrau region and the Cicerone team who have done their
(absolutely normal) great job to make a great guidebook.*

Updates to this guide

While every effort is made by our authors to ensure the accuracy of
guidebooks as they go to print, changes can occur during the lifetime of an
edition. Any updates that we know of for this guide will be on the Cicerone
website (www.cicerone.co.uk/1114/updates), so please check before
planning your trip. We also advise that you check information about such
things as transport, accommodation and shops locally. Even rights of way
can be altered over time. We are always grateful for information about any
discrepancies between a guidebook and the facts on the ground, sent by
email to updates@cicerone.co.uk or by post to Cicerone, Juniper House,
Murley Moss, Oxenholme Road, Kendal, LA9 7RL.

Register your book: To sign up to receive free updates, special offers
and GPX files where available, register your book in your Cicerone library
at www.cicerone.co.uk.

Front cover: Grindelwald and its mountains — the Schreckhorn and Wetterhorn

CONTENTS

Mountain safety

Every mountain walk has its dangers, and those described in this guidebook are no exception. All who walk or climb in the mountains should recognise this and take responsibility for themselves and their companions along the way. The author and publisher have made every effort to ensure that the information contained in this guide was correct when it went to press, but, except for any liability that cannot be excluded by law, they cannot accept responsibility for any loss, injury or inconvenience sustained by any person using this book.

International distress signal *(emergency only)*
Six blasts on a whistle (and flashes with a torch after dark) spaced evenly for one minute, followed by a minute's pause. Repeat until an answer is received. The response is three signals per minute followed by a minute's pause.

Helicopter rescue
The following signals are used to communicate with a helicopter:

Help needed: raise both arms above head to form a 'Y'

Help not needed: raise one arm above head, extend other arm downward

Emergency telephone numbers
If telephoning from the UK the dialling code is: 0041
Switzerland: Accident Services tel 144
Europe-wide: Emergency tel 112

Weather reports
Switzerland: tel 162 (in French, German or Italian), www.meteoschweiz.ch/en

Mountain rescue can be very expensive – be adequately insured.

Symbols used on route maps

~~	route
- - -	alternative route
Ⓢ	start point
Ⓕ	finish point
ⓈⒻ	start/finish point
ⓈⒻ	alternative start/finish point
Ⓕ	alternative finish point
➤	route direction
	glacier
	woodland
	urban areas
▬▬■▬▬	station/railway
P	parking
■	bus stop/station
🚠 🚡 🚟	cable car/gondola car/chair lift
▲	peak
⬆ ⇧	manned/unmanned refuge
⇧	other accommodation
M	museum
🍴	refreshment
🚻	public toilets
■	building
☆	point of interest
≍ =	col/bridge
⸙ •	waterfall/water feature
⼝	picnic area
✱	viewpoint
•	other feature

Relief
in metres

4200 and above
4000–4200
3800–4000
3600–3800
3400–3600
3200–3400
3000–3200
2800–3000
2600–2800
2400–2600
2200–2400
2000–2200
1800–2000
1600–1800
1400–1600
1200–1400
1000–1200
800–1000
600–800
400–600
200–400
0–200

Maps are at 1:50,000 unless otherwise stated.

SCALE: 1:50,000

0 kilometres 0.5		1
0 miles	0.5	

Contour lines are drawn at 25m intervals and highlighted at 100m intervals.

GPX files for all routes can be downloaded free at www.cicerone.co.uk/1114/GPX.

The awesome wall of the Gspaltenhorn overlooks the entire Sefinental valley (Walk 44)

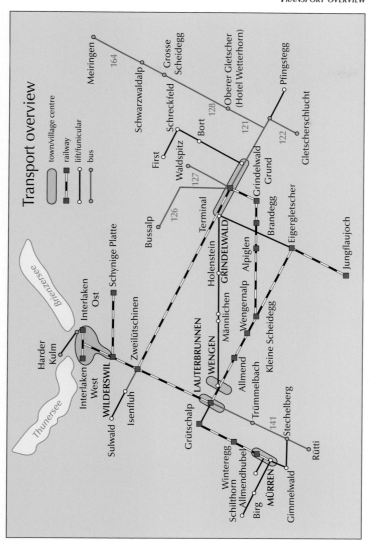

Transport overview

- ⬭ town/village centre
- ▮ railway
- ▮ lift/funicular
- ○ bus

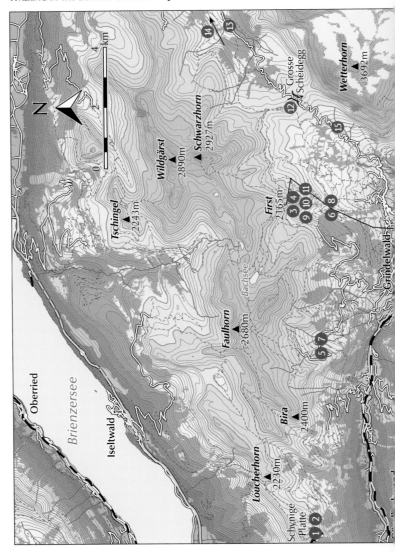

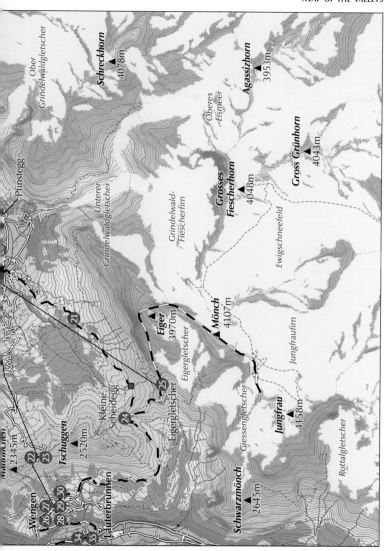

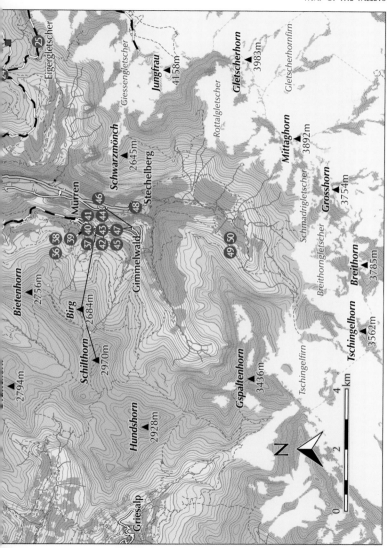

ROUTE SUMMARY TABLE

Route	Area and Route	Highlights	Distance km	Ascent m	Descent m	Grade (1–4)	Time Hr/min	Page
Schynige Platte to First								
1	Schynige Platte Panoramaweg	Views, alpine garden	5.5	225	225	2	1hr 45min	44
2	Schynige Platte – Faulhorn – First	Views, high hut	16	950	750	3	5hr 30min	47
3	First – Bachsee – Faulhorn – Bussalp	Bachsee, high traverse, hut, views	10.5	560	930	2–3	4hr	52
4	First – Spitzen – Bussalp – the Höhenweg 2200	Interesting ridge crossing	8.75	310	680	2	3hr	55
5	Bussalp – Waldspitz – First – the Höhenweg 2000	Views, mountain restaurants	12	790	420	2	4hr 30min	59
6	Bort to Bussalp – the Höhenweg 1600	Views, easy walking, restaurants	7.5	390	155	1	2hr 15min	63
7	Bussalp to Grindelwald	Views, easy walking, waterfall	6	15	770	1	1hr 45min	66
8	Bort – Alpenvogelpark – Hotel Wetterhorn	Views, waterfall, alpine bird park	6	180	510	1–2	1hr 45min	69
9	First – Grosse Scheidegg – Hotel Wetterhorn – Grindelwald	Views, classic downhill walk, restaurants	14	120	1240	1–2	3hr 45min	72
10	First – Bachsee – Waldspitz	Views, mountain lake, restaurants	6.5	150	420	1–2	2hr	77
11	The Schwarzhorn Circuit: First – Wart – Grosse Scheidegg	Remote, rewarding mountain challenge	14.5	800	1000	3	5hr	82
Grosse Scheidegg and Meiringen								
12	Grosse Scheidegg to Schwarzwaldalp	Views, picnic area, easy walking, restaurant	9	90	600	2	2hr 30min	88
13	The Rychenbach valley: Schwarzwaldalp – Rosenlaui circuit	Views, riverside walk, option to visit gorge, traditional sawmill	6.75	170	170	1	2hr	91
14	Meiringen – Grosse Scheidegg – Grindelwald on the Via Alpina	Quiet valley, classic through-route, Reichenbach waterfalls	23.5	1440	1000	2	8hr	95

Route	Area and Route	Highlights	Distance km	Ascent m	Descent m	Grade (1-4)	Time Hr/min	Page
Routes into the mountain wall								
15	The Gleckstein Hut	Hut overlooking glacier, difficult terrain, views	10.5	900	1230	4	5hr	102
16	Grindelwald – Pfingstegg – Hotel Wetterhorn circuit	Gorge, restaurants, views	14	680	680	2	4hr 30min	105
17	Pfingstegg – Bäregg Hut	Hut overlooking glacier, superb views	5.5	460	460	2-3	3hr	108
18	The Schreckhorn Hut	Close views of Finsteraarhorn, challenging	16	1660	1660	4	10hr	112
Grindelwald to Kleine Scheidegg								
19	Grindelwald – Kleine Scheidegg – Wengen – Lauterbrunnen	Classic views, restaurants, train options	19	1120	1270	2	6–7hr	116
20	Grindelwald to Alpiglen the hard way	Exposed dramatic route, restaurant	9.25	880	300	3	4hr	121
21	The Eiger Trail – Alpiglen to Eigergletscher and Kleine Scheidegg	Views, dramatic situation under Eiger north face	6	780	80/340	2-3	3– 3hr 30min	124
22	Männlichen to Alpiglen, the Romantic Way – the Höhenweg 1900	Eiger north face views, restaurants	7.5	40	645	2	2hr	128
23	Männlichen to Kleine Scheidegg Panoramaweg – the Höhenweg 2100	Mountain views, easy walking	4.5	20	180	1	1hr	132
Wengen to Kleine Scheidegg								
24	Kleine Scheidegg and Wengernalp	Views to Mürren, woods and meadows, restaurants	10	460	460	2	3hr 30min	136
25	Eigergletscher to Wengen by the moraine	Dramatic situation and views, restaurants	11.5	100	1150	2-3	3hr 30min	139

Route	Area and Route	Highlights	Distance km	Ascent m	Descent m	Grade (1–4)	Time Hr/min	Page
26	Wengen – Leiterhorn circuit	Wooded hillsides, views, BBQ picnic area	5.25	240	240	2	1hr 45min	144
27	Wengen to Männlichen – the Gemsweg	Steep well-made path with views	5	950	0	3	3hr	147
28	Wengen and the Mendelssohn memorial	Memorial, best Lauterbrunnen viewpoints	5	250	250	1	1hr 30min	150
29	Wengen – Stalden – Allmend – Wengen	Woodlands, views, restaurants	10	425	425	2	3hr	153
30	The Trümmelbach falls: Wengen – Stalden – Trümmelbach	Woodlands, views, upper canyon, steep aided route	10	460	920	3	3hr 30min	157
Lauterbrunnen and Isenfluh								
31	Saxeten to Isenfluh	Traverse to Lauterbrunnen valley, hut with views	14	980	1000	2–3	5hr 15min	162
32	Sulwald to Mürren by the Lobhorn Hut	Fine mountain hut and superb views	14	920	800	2	5hr 15min	166
33	Grütschalp to Sulwald	Woodland walk, quiet valleys, fine views	6.5	400	360	2	2hr 20min	171
34	Lauterbrunnen, Trümmelbach Falls and Stechelberg	Valley walk and spectacular falls inside mountain	7.5	150	40	1	2hr	174
35	Lauterbrunnen to Mürren on the Via Alpina	Wooded climb to Mürren	6.5	850	10	2	2hr 45min	177
Mürren								
36	The Mountain View Trail to Grütschalp	Views of Eiger Mönch and Jungfrau	5.5	110	530	2	1hr 45min	182
37	Mürren, the Blumental and Chänelegg	Easy walk, views and unspoilt nature	6	335	335	1–2	2hr	185

Route	Area and Route	Highlights	Distance km	Ascent m	Descent m	Grade (1-4)	Time Hr/min	Page
38	The North Face Trail – Allmendhubel to Mürren via Schiltalp	Mountain inns and fine views	6.5	180	450	1–2	2hr 10min	188
39	The 'easy' way up the Schilthorn from Allmendhubel	So-called easy way up the Schilthorn	6.5	1085	25	3	3hr 30min	192
40	The Schilthorn via Schiltalp and Grauseewli	Best way up the Schilthorn	8	1360	30	3	4hr	196
41	Mürren – Gimmelwald – Mürren	Quiet village walk in shadow of Jungfrau	5	300	300	1–2	1hr 45min	199
42	Mürren to the Stutz waterfall and Spielbodenalp	A great waterfall	7.5	360	360	2	2hr 30min	202
43	Mürren, Bryndli and the Rotstock Hut	Exciting ascent, panoramic views and a great hut	13.5	720	720	3	5hr	206
44	The Sefinental and Rotstock Hut	Beautiful secluded valley and great hut	15	840	840	2–3	5hr 15min	209
45	Mürren to Griesalp on the Via Alpina	Crossing the area's hardest walkers' col	16.5	1020	1250	3	7hr	213

Stechelberg and Upper Lauterbrunnen valley

Route	Area and Route	Highlights	Distance km	Ascent m	Descent m	Grade (1-4)	Time Hr/min	Page
46	Stechelberg – Gimmelwald – Mürren	Wooden climb and quiet villages	6.5	800	25	1–2	3hr	220
47	Mürren to Obersteinberg via the Tanzbödeli	Beautiful route to inns and peaceful valley	9	950	810	3	4hr 15min	223
48	Stechelberg to Obersteinberg	Exploring quiet valley and climb to inns	8.5	890	20	2	3hr 15min	227
49	Obersteinberg – Oberhornsee – Stechelberg	Unspoilt mountain lake in alpine area and fine views	11	420	1290	2	4hr 30min	230
50	Obersteinberg – Oberhornsee – Schmadri Hut – Stechelberg	Mountain lake and remote hut on a high alpine walk	13	680	1550	3	5hr 30min	236

Superb views into the Lauterbrunnen valley from just above the Schynige Platte (Walk 1)

INTRODUCTION

Eiger, Mönch and Jungfrau from Schynige Platte (Walk 1)

Dawn breaks, and the uppermost tip of the Eiger glows amber, while wispy pillows of cloud still linger in the valley, partly obscuring the hillside below Männlichen and Kleine Scheidegg. The villages are waking to another fine day, the first rays of sun catching terraces festooned with bright geraniums, while the smell of fresh bread and coffee fills the air. The day will be good, and there will be fine views – some of the most awe-inspiring views in the whole of the Alps, and there will be great walking – striding out on good paths, with mountain inns to visit, and trains and cable cars easing tired legs back to the villages below.

While the Eiger, Mönch and Jungfrau together form the iconic wall of rock and ice towering over the settlements of Grindelwald, Wengen and Mürren, there are more shapely and higher peaks to admire too, including the Schreckhorn, Finsteraarhorn and Fiescherhorn. The Wetterhorn stands as a powerful and distinctive guardian at the eastern end of the Jungfrau region looming high above Grosse Scheidegg – the high pass leading directly down to Grindelwald.

Below these mighty rock faces lies a world of rich green pastures, studded by glimmering lakes creating reflections that double the impressive

views. Good mountain paths lead to lesser peaks and impressive ridges, while mountaineers revel in the challenges that the high mountains offer. Cascading mountain streams cut deep gorges, and some of Europe's most impressive waterfalls fall 300m or more, like great lace curtains into the Lauterbrunnen valley. There are easier paths too, threading through larch and pine woodlands, or easing along panoramic balcony routes between inviting mountain restaurants and refuges, most in fantastic locations providing the opportunity to linger and admire the view at your leisure. In short, this is a Swiss chocolate box with varieties for everyone!

Grindelwald is the largest of the three main holiday villages covered in this guide, occupying a grassy hillside at just over 1000m altitude directly facing the impressive mountain wall of the Eiger, with the rising hillside between Kleine Scheidegg and Männlichen opposite. It's a friendly resort, still holding strong farming connections and traditions, with local artisan produce readily available, and festivals celebrating the seasons. Thanks to its position as a major ski resort there is an impressive modern infrastructure of lift systems and railways to speedily transport walkers to higher ground from where many of the routes either start or finish, but fear not – there is little evidence of ski pistes to worry you or to scar the landscape. Grindelwald has additional attractions including a good sports centre, the impressive Gletscherschlucht Gorge, a small but worthwhile museum, and options to rent scooters on which to zoom down the hillside from Bort back to Grindelwald.

Basking on a sunny terrace on the western side of the Lauterbrunnen valley, **Mürren** is the highest of the three main resorts at around 1600m, with impressive views directly to the great mountain wall stretching from the Eiger westwards to beyond the Breithorn. Mürren has an excellent infrastructure of lifts linking Stechelberg in the lower valley up to the Schilthorn (aka Piz Gloria of James Bond fame), via Gimmelwald and Mürren. Entirely car-free, the village is also accessed from Lauterbrunnen via a cable car and a special train from Grütschalp. Although smaller than Grindelwald, Mürren also has its own sports centre, and other attractions include the little hamlet of Gimmelwald perched on the very edge of the cliff above the Lauterbrunnen valley, where traditional farming practices are normal, and where 21st-century tourism has had little influence.

Occupying a sloping sunny terrace on the eastern side of the Lauterbrunnen valley, much of car-free **Wengen** enjoys superb views south to the magnificent mountain wall of the central Bernese Oberland, but also deep into the Lauterbrunnen valley and across to Mürren. The village is accessed from both Lauterbrunnen and Grindelwald by the mountain railway system leading to Kleine Scheidegg. More developed than Mürren, Wengen lies at just over 1200m and has been favoured for decades by alpine walkers and explorers including composer Felix Mendelssohn, who found peace and inspiration among these mountains.

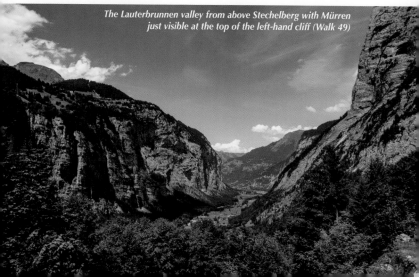

The Lauterbrunnen valley from above Stechelberg with Mürren just visible at the top of the left-hand cliff (Walk 49)

For those seeking quieter locations to base themselves, there are smaller hamlets and chalets dotted on the hillsides, many with good access, just fewer people and amenities! This area is indeed a delight, and a near-perfect part of the Alps for the adventurous walker.

EIGER, MÖNCH AND JUNGFRAU

Although known by tourists throughout the world as the Jungfrau Region, mainly due to the amazing railway to the Jungfraujoch, it is the Eiger at 3967m (meaning Ogre), and its impressive 1800m near-vertical north face that has attracted the world's leading mountaineers over many generations. The first ascent of the Eiger was made in 1858 by Swiss guides Christian Almer and Peter Bohren and an Irishman Charles Barrington, while the north face was only conquered by an Austrian–German expedition in 1938. *The White Spider* is a classic work of mountain literature giving a harrowing account of the first ascent of the north face in 1938 by the author Heinrich Harrer and other members of the team – Anderl Heckmair, Ludwig Vörg and Fritz Kasparek. Many climbers have lost their lives before and since, making an attempt on the north face, most losing their lives when climbing during the summer months. Summer ascents via the Mittellegi Ridge are considered easier, but all are difficult.

The mountain by which the area is better known is the elegant Jungfrau (meaning maiden, or virgin) at 4158m, first climbed in 1811 by the Meyer brothers and two hunters from the Valais. In summer, walkers who take the train to the Jungfraujoch can enjoy an excellent walk up the Jungfrau glacier as far as the Obers Mönchsjoch at 3623m, then for refreshments at the Mönchsjochhütte above.

Sandwiched between these iconic mountains is another giant, the Mönch (meaning Monk) at 4,110m, with the prominent Eiger Glacier separating it from the Eiger.

THE SHAPE OF THE MOUNTAINS

The Bernese Alps lie to the north of the Rhône valley and stretch from the end of the Uri Alps at the Grimsel Pass in the east, through to the Chablais Alps and Martigny where the Rhône forces its way between these mountain ranges.

The Engelhörner group of mountains lie between Meiringen and Grindelwald, which although lower than the giant neighbours to the south, are very distinctive, with towering peaks and slabs and the remnants of glaciers high above. Then follows the Wetterhorn, a huge bulky mountain with multiple summits acting as guardian to the main area covered in this guide, and together with its neighbour the Mättenberg, is visible from most of the walks from Grindelwald

The Schreckhorn, distant Finsteraahorn and Fiescherhorn from the classic view at Bachsee (Walk 3)

and Kleine Scheidegg, while the Gleckstein Hut occupies the space between, and is a popular outing for more experienced mountain walkers, and climbers.

The Bernese giants Eiger, Mönch and Jungfrau follow in succession, but less visible is the Finsteraarhorn (4274m), the highest in the Bernese Oberland, the Schreckhorn and Fiescherhorn among others, which can be seen at close quarters from the Schreckhorn Hut, another challenging route for the experienced. For those less willing or able to undertake a challenging mountain route, these superb peaks can be seen from many of the walks which explore the hillsides of Bussalp, Bachsee and the Faulhorn, as well as from Schynige Platte. From these easily accessed viewpoints, the entire magnificent range is laid out before you in a

dazzling panorama of rock and ice which scratches the (often) deep blue sky, with the greenest of pastures lying far below.

From the Jungfrau west the mountain chain includes, in order, the Gletcherhorn, Mittaghorn, Grosshorn, Breithorn and Tschingelhorn. The Blümlisalp and Gspaltenhorn lie to the west above the Rotstock Hut and Sefinafurgga, while the Schilthorn is also clearly visible within the more extensive Schynige Platte panorama.

Several impressive glaciers carve their way through the range, the most impressive being the Aletsch glacier which originates in a vast snowfield to the south of the Mönch and Jungfrau near the Jungfraujoch, part of the Jungfrau-Aletsch UNESCO World Heritage Site. It then flows in a huge loop south and west down to the Rhône, enclosed on the northern side by the giants of the Bernese Alps, and to the south by a minor ridge finishing at Eggishorn.

The Alps are relatively young 'fold mountains', having formed between 40 and 25 million years ago when the African and Eurasian plates collided, compressing and folding the continental crust and forcing both plates upwards while most of the African plate slid over the top. The Eurasian plate consisted of light crystalline rocks much of which sank to a depth of around 25km. The continued pressure forced the remaining Eurasian plate up to the surface at a steep angle. It is this steep angle, together with the subsequent glacial erosion, that has resulted in the steep north faces of the main range.

Peaks over 4000m in the Bernese Oberland:

- Finsteraarhorn 4274m
- Aletschhorn 4182m
- Jungfrau 4166m
- Mönch 4105m
- Schreckhorn 4080m
- Grosses Fiescherhorn 4049m
- Grünhorn 4043m
- Lauteraarhorn 4042m
- Hinteres Fiescherhorn 4025m

There are a further 40 peaks in the Bernese Oberland over 3500m in height, including the Eiger (3967m), the Lauterbrunnen Breithorn (3779m) and the Wetterhorn (3708m).

THE MAIN CENTRES AND VALLEYS

From the glaciers and sparkling snowy peaks, the water of the Lütchine river flows towards Interlaken. Grindelwald occupies a sunny sloping bowl of green pasture at the head of the Schwarze (Black) branch of the river, the Lütschental to the east, while the Weisse (white) branch of the river flows though the Lauterbrunnen valley. The two branches of the river join at Zweilütschinen (two Lütschine rivers), as do the railway and road networks.

Of the three main resorts in the region, Grindelwald is the largest and most accessible, while Wengen and Mürren, the smaller car-free resorts, are perched in high hanging valleys on either side of the Lauterbrunnen valley. From each of these main resorts there is a superb network of mountain trains, lifts, cable cars and buses (for Grindelwald and the Lauterbrunnen valley), to take you up to many high points and mountain restaurants from which many of the walks begin, or end.

The walks range from straightforward strolls on wide, near-level paths and tracks, through to exposed and challenging mountain routes, and longer through-routes. However, the majority of the walks described are day walks using well-marked (yellow or red and white signage) mountain hiking paths to visit mountain huts, lakes, cols, viewpoints and a few easy peaks.

In late spring and autumn, the tightly-knit farming communities still celebrate the passing of the seasons with festivals and parades – the sight of the cows making their way proudly down from the high pastures resplendent in their festival headdresses and ceremonial bells is a memorable sight, and sound!

Linguistically the language is German, or more accurately Schweizerdeutsch, although if you speak high German (hochdeutsch) you will be understood. English tends to be well understood, the region being particularly popular with English-speaking visitors. Occasionally local signpost and map spellings may diverge and cause some confusion, however the local spellings are usually identifiably close.

Grindelwald

Sheltered on nearly all sides by mountains, the resort of Grindelwald feels welcoming and safe, yet hugely inspiring for walkers and climbers to explore the mountains. Its long main street is filled with shops, hotels and restaurants to suit most budgets, while to both the north and south lie a network of roads and green terraces scattered with chalets and barns. Until the late 18th century the area was

Autumn parade in Grindelwald

entirely devoted to pasture for cattle, with some fruit and vegetable farming nearest to the village.

Glaciers in the region dominated the area, the Unterer and Oberer Grindelwald glaciers extended into the valley beyond the Gletscherschlucht gorge as recently as 1864. During the 19th century people became interested in the landscape and mountains, and the two accessible glaciers at Grindelwald attracted many visitors, sparking the development of the railway and hotels, and the development of Grindelwald as a resort. The gorge makes a fine excursion and can be included in the Pfingstegg walk. Today the valley is dominated by farming during the summer months, where cows graze the high alp pastures, and trees hang heavy with fruit in the vestiges of orchards in and around the village.

Grindelwald offers the most diverse walking. The high pass of Grosse Scheidegg provides the main gateway from Meiringen, with easy riverside walking exploring around Schwarzwaldalp and the gorge at Rosenlaui in the Rychenbach valley. Three longer walks describe sections of the long-distance walking route Via Alpina 1 as it passes through the area covered in this guide, leading from Meiringen over Grosse Scheidegg to Grindelwald, then on to Mürren and finally Griesalp in the west.

The mountainside to the north of Grindelwald between Schynige Platte and Grosse Scheidegg is covered with a lattice of mountain paths and tracks all enjoying superb views of the massive mountain wall of Wetterhorn, Eiger, Mönch and Jungfrau, with many of the routes starting or finishing on the way to, or at the First gondola station. Most are either graded as hiking trails or Wanderweg (with yellow signage) or mountain hiking trails or Bergwanderweg (with red and white signage), so are suitable for most abilities.

To the south and west many more paths can be accessed using the Männlichen and Eigergletscher lift systems and the mountain railway to Kleine Scheidegg, including access from the Eigergletscher station to the Jungfraujoch and the renowned Eiger Trail, and the Panoramaweg and Romanticweg from Männlichen. The routes provide fairly straightforward walking, although some routes such as routes to the Gleckstein and Schreckhorn Huts have more exposure than others.

Wengen

Wengen is situated on a high terrace 400m above the Lauterbrunnen valley at an altitude of just over 1200m. Once a small farming alp settlement, the advent of the railway from Lauterbrunnen in 1893 allowed this pretty mountain village to develop into a popular resort for both winter and summer activities. It is known that the composer Mendelssohn loved the area and stayed on several occasions in order to enjoy fresh mountain air,

Chalets, pastures and orchards on the edge of Wengen

peace and inspiration. A memorial in the woods to the north of the village marks the location from which he sketched the Jungfrau. Today the village makes an ideal quiet base for a walking holiday, with good access to all parts of the region via the Lauterbrunnen and Klein Scheidegg mountain railway and the Männlichen cable car.

Wengen is surrounded by a superb network of mainly woodland paths sloping up to the Leiterhorn in the north and towards Stalden in the south, with a more challenging route – the Gemsweg directly up to Männlichen. The railway provides additional options for further exploration from stations on the way to Kleine Scheidegg, and the cable car to Männlichen can speedily connect with other routes to the north. The resort also enjoys an enviable record of sunshine.

Mürren

Situated on a sunny terrace at a slightly loftier height of around 1600m on the western side of the Lauterbrunnen valley lies Mürren, an equally popular resort. This is an ideal centre from which to enjoy the labyrinth of mountain paths rising towards the Schilthorn at 2971m, as well as paths to the north including the Lobhorn, and westwards to the Sefinafurgga pass leading to Griesalp. Perhaps the greatest gem for adventurous walkers based in Mürren is easy access to the upper Lauterbrunnen valley, known as the Hinteres Lauterbrunnental, a protected area of outstanding beauty. Smaller and with fewer facilities, car-free Mürren is generally considered to be a quieter resort, with fantastic views from almost anywhere, giving a feeling of hanging in the sky just below the mighty Jungfrau. There are a few more lift options up to, and above Mürren, to start more challenging walks from a higher point including an ascent of the Schilthorn and various high passes in the area. A funicular rises from the centre of the village to Allmendhubel, a leisure area enjoying superb views and easy walking opportunities, while other less-demanding walks lead to mountain restaurants, waterfalls and to the traditional hamlet of Gimmelwald.

At the time of writing, a new cable car is under construction to run directly from Stechelberg to Mürren, with a connection to Birg and the Schilthorn. We understand that the cable car via Gimmelwald will continue to operate until at least 2030.

Smaller villages including Gimmelwald and Isenfluh offer a limited range of accommodation so provide a quieter base from which to explore; Gimmelwald is reached by cable car from Stechelberg, and Isenfluh by bus from Lauterbrunnen. Perched high above Interlaken and accessed by bus, Saxeten also has options for accommodation in a quieter village setting.

Lauterbrunnen valley

The Lauterbrunnen valley (meaning 'many fountains') is easily accessible and is renowned for the 72 spectacular waterfalls which cascade elegantly in drops of 300m from both sides of this impressive classic 'U' shaped glacial-carved valley. Good riverside pastures have been used for centuries by the farmers in the valley, while at the head of the valley above Rütti and Stechelberg is the Hinteres Lauterbrunnental, one of the biggest nature conservation areas in Switzerland. Protected from both Hydro and tourist development, the area is drained by multiple streams and waterfalls cascading from the glaciers which still cling to the slopes of the great wall of mountains that surround the upper valley. Three mountain inns and a high hut provide options to explore and make the most of the fine walking opportunities.

PLANTS AND WILDLIFE

For much of the year the alpine slopes are covered with snow. The blanket of snow acts as protection for hardy little plants, providing shelter from harsh winds, insulation from the bitter cold, and moisture while the plants rest in a semi-hibernation state. All this changes as soon as the snow begins to melt, with myriad varieties of alpine flowers blooming in succession in the short summer season. The first to appear is the alpine snowbell (*Soldanella*), with tiny, fringed pink/purple flowers supported on thin stems. In June more plants come into flower, mainly pink and purple in colour including *Anemone*, *Gentian*, Alpine snowbell, Globeflower and

Summer flower meadows near Mürren

Auricula. In July the Alpenrose transforms many of the hillsides in the area into a sea of vivid rose red. This slow-growing plant takes its time but can colonise huge areas of both open hillside and lightly shaded woodland. Autumn sees many of the hillsides turn a different shade, as thousands of blueberry (*myrtille*) bushes take on their incredible autumn colour. The alpine garden at Schynige Platte is home to over 750 species of alpine flower, offers guided tours and is highly recommended. A mini-guide by Gillian Price '*Alpine Flowers*' is published by Cicerone.

The area covered in this guidebook is extremely popular with walkers and mountain visitors during the summer months, which sadly means that the likelihood of encountering native mountain wildlife is limited. Higher remote altitudes provide mountain refuges for Ibex and Chamois, and there is a chance that you will spot these wonderful creatures if tackling the more difficult higher and less visited routes. Chamois have short, slender horns, and tend to live and feed in small family groups, while ibex have longer, thicker ridged horns.

Take a walk across a high alpine meadow and you may hear a piercing whistle repeated over and over again. Locate where the sound is coming from, and you should see a small brown rodent, about the size of a mountain hare, standing upright sounding the alarm. These shy creatures are marmots; they graze on vegetation in the high alps and live in burrows underground where they hibernate during the winter months.

Meanwhile on the lower slopes and in woodland, you may be lucky to spot tiny red-black squirrels scuttling around at great speed, foraging for berries and vegetation.

The skies are the preserve of the Alpine chough, a close relative of the crow, and eagles can often be spotted riding the thermals high above the hillsides.

WHEN TO GO

The main walking season runs from mid-June until mid-September. Outside this period, huts may well not be open and much of the other accommodation may also be closed. June, July and August tend to be the hottest months, but this can also tend to lead to evening thunderstorms. The weather is often unsettled in late August as the temperatures cool, however, September and October can be more settled. Daytime temperatures are ideal for walking, cooling progressively at night, and with autumn colour emerging, these are attractive months to visit, and although accommodation and restaurants will progressively close over the period, the walking can be outstanding well into October.

Grindelwald claims to enjoy 300 days per year of sunshine. However, high in the mountains, local factors may have a greater impact on the weather. Hot air rising from the valleys can bring storms, and the normal Alpine thunderstorms of late afternoon may occur throughout the summer, particularly on humid days. And if a low-pressure zone settles over southern Switzerland, it could be dreary for a day or two. Heatwaves affecting the rest of Europe also affect this area, but the altitude and the dryness of the mountain air make them more manageable. The north-facing wall of the Bernese Oberland acts as a magnet for incoming weather systems so storms may linger high in the mountains for a couple of days.

In June and well into July, there may be late-lying snow above 2000m. Snow can fall at any time higher in the mountains during the summer but will usually melt very quickly during the day. Check conditions before arriving – there are many webcams, so it is possible to inspect the mountainsides directly. Tourist offices will have a clear if perhaps cautious view on which routes are open. In the summer, late-lying snow will be soft and frustrating. In more exposed places, however, often on north-facing slopes and other sheltered places where there is less direct sunshine, it is possible to come across hard snow (*névé*) or even ice, so look out for this and unless you are equipped with axe, crampons and poles take another route.

Temperature and rainfall statistics for Grindelwald over the summer months are shown in the table, with an average of over 200 hours of sunshine expected in June.

Month	Average high (°C)	Average rainfall (mm)
May	20	125
June	22	140
July	25	145
August	24	150
September	20	100
October	15	70

Source: weather-and-climate.com
Interlaken weather station data

GETTING THERE

Switzerland is very accessible and has an excellent public transport infrastructure. The central Bernese Oberland is, however, some distance from the main airports or access points into the country, so it is likely that it will take at least two to three hours to reach your chosen resort after first entering Switzerland.

By train

From the UK the trip by rail will cost a little more and take a little longer than flying, but it is perfectly feasible as well as more environmentally friendly. From London St Pancras take the Eurostar to Paris Gare du Nord, then either two stops in Paris on the RER (green line D) to the Gare du Lyon for trains to Geneva and Lausanne, or head to Gare de L'Est then take the TGV from Paris, changing onto Swiss trains at Basel then on to Interlaken Ost. (Other routes avoiding Paris are available.)

From Interlaken there are trains up to Grindelwald and to Lauterbrunnen (for Mürren and Wengen). London to

The First gondola lift at Grindelwald

Walkers beside the track between Grütschalp and Mürren

Interlaken can be booked on a single ticket through French railways (SNCF), but it may be worth splitting the booking to take advantage of discount deals and cards on both the French and Swiss railways.

At Interlaken, board a train to Lauterbrunnen/Grindelwald, and try to make sure you are at the right end of the train for your destination, as the trains split at Zweilütschinen, one half continuing south to Lauterbrunnen, the other half heading up towards Grindelwald. Note that Grindelwald Terminal station links the Männlichen and Eigergletscher gondola lifts and is NOT the final stop, which is in the village a few minutes further on.

Rail journeys from Belgium and the Netherlands and other points in northern Europe are also options and often shorter.

By road

Road access is through the French motorway system via Metz and Strasbourg, or via Nancy to Basel and Bern, or further south to Bern via Troyes. You will need a Swiss motorway vignette (sticker), which currently costs £45 and is available online or CHF40 at the Swiss border.

By air

Switzerland's main airports are Geneva and Zurich. From each of these it is possible to book trains right through to Grindelwald and Lauterbrunnen (around 4 hours from Geneva airport and roughly 3 hours from Zurich). Geneva and Zurich are served by both low-cost and full-service airlines within Europe, from the UK and internationally. For flight information visit www.skyscanner.net and www.kayak.co.uk.

Discounts

Many often-complex discounts are available for Swiss trains, buses and cable cars, giving substantial savings. See 'Discount Cards and Passes', and Appendix B.

TRAVEL IN THE REGION

Cable cars, mountain railways, funiculars, gondolas and chairlifts are an integral part of the Alpine walking experience, and the network available in the region is extensive, possibly the best in the whole of the Alps (See Transport map). Many can be discounted by using various discount cards and tickets. (See Appendix B.)

Post buses offer regular services at least hourly, and often more frequently within the Grindelwald area. There are frequent bus services to locations north and south above Grindelwald, including from Meiringen via Grosse Scheidegg. A bus service also operates from Lauterbrunnen south to Stechelberg.

Mountain trains carry passengers from Grindelwald Grund station up to Alpiglen then on to Kleine Scheidegg with options to board the train to the Jungfraujoch – one of the highlights of the entire area, via Eigergletscher. Kleine Scheidegg is also the terminus for the mountain train from Lauterbrunnen, via Wengen and various other stops on the route.

Grindelwald Terminal feels more like a modern airport, with a new lift to Männlichen, the impressive 'tricable' lift to Eigergletcher (linking with the Jungfraujoch train) and trains to Interlaken, or Grindelwald village. The gondola lift from Grindelwald to First is a useful route, popular in summer providing easy access to numerous walks above Grindelwald, while lifts above Mürren and Wengen can extend the scope of day walking. Full details of discount cards and additional options for each resort are described below.

DISCOUNT CARDS AND PASSES

A wide range of Swiss Travel passes are available to the visitor, each offering a different combination of coverage. It's complicated! Take time to consider exactly what your expected travel plans are in Switzerland and buy the most appropriate pass. In most cases a pass is the most economic option if you intend to use public transport of any sort, and while trains and buses tend to be less expensive, lifts and mountain railways are costly without any kind of discount.

If you plan to spend more than two or three weeks travelling by rail to, and within Switzerland, then the best option is probably to buy a **Swiss Half Fare Travel Card**, which is valid for either a month, or a whole year for if you plan multiple trips. To buy and use it, you will need to apply for a **Swiss Pass** and download the Swiss Travel app. Once you have a customer number and account, the app will allow you to purchase all eligible tickets at the discounted price automatically. The application and purchase is probably easiest made by post.

Easier options for a single trip of between 3 and 15 days are outlined in a table in Appendix B, in each case we have tried to identify the main advantages and suitability for the holiday planned. Details and options change from year to year, so you should check details of all options, and make your preferred purchase on the main Swiss Travel website: shop. switzerlandtravelcentre.com.

In virtually every case, it is better value to get a discount card than to pay as you go. Lifts and mountain railways are essential in order to make the most of the walking opportunities in the area. For example, many return tickets cost around CHF65, and a return to the Jungfraujoch is CHF220 full price.

If you want to maximise free travel using all transport including lifts and mountain railways in the entire Bernese Oberland region, including some special discounts, then the **Bernese Oberland Regional Pass** is excellent value, and also offers half price fares from the Swiss border to the Bernese Oberland region, but it excludes the Jungfraujoch and Schilthorn.

For visitors staying for a week or less, the **Top of Europe Pass** is good value, with unlimited free travel on all the lifts, mountain railways and railways south of Interlaken, plus one

trip to the Jungfraujoch, while the **Jungfrau Travel Pass** also includes lake ferry trips, but only a discount for the Jungfraujoch.

Local resort **Guest Cards** also provide free services and discounts. All resort digital guest cards provide discounts of around 30% for lifts from both sides of Männlichen and the train to Schynige Platte, plus other discounts on local facilities including minigolf, tennis and swimming. In addition, with the Grindelwald guest card discounts are available on the First gondola lift and, in summer, on the cable car to Pfingstegg, the glacier gorge and the Hellbach outdoor pool. The town bus services are free, however the card does not cover the mountain bus service to Grosse Scheidegg or to Bussalp.

A summary of the main lifts and their current opening periods and running times is provided in Appendix B.

ACCOMMODATION

A wide range of good accommodation is available throughout the region. There are outstanding tourist offices in each village who will gladly assist in finding and booking accommodation in both hotels and apartments, as well as helpful websites (see Appendix A), to help the visitor choose the most suitable options.

Camping

There are four campsites in the Grindelwald valley and three in the

Berghaus Männdlenen (Walk 2)

Lauterbrunnen valley (see Appendix A). Prices vary but are generally between CHF10 and CHF15 plus a tourist tax of CHF3–5 per person per night, and between CHF10 and CHF15 for a pitch for your tent. With plentiful local restaurants as well as supermarkets, this is a good, low-cost option.

Apartments

As these centres are also busy winter resorts, there are many apartments available to rent in the summer. Prices may be around CHF1000 per week or more for very good 2-bedroom, 4-person apartments. Mürren and Wengen can be a little more expensive.

Hotels

There is a wide range of hotels, from the simple to the height of luxury, details of which are available through the tourist offices or directly online.

Huts and berghotels (mountain inns)

It is quite possible to use mountain huts and other mountain accommodation as a base for a few days. Mountain huts (*Hütte*) are either operated by the Swiss Alpine Club (SAC) or are privately owned. A *berghotel* (or *berggasthaus*) is privately run, often offering more private accommodation, but still providing communal sleeping in dormitories (*lager*), as well as private rooms. Overnight stays will usually cost in the range of CHF70–90 per person, including dinner and breakfast. All will provide a picnic lunch, if requested in good time, at an additional cost. A full list can be found in Appendix A, including suggestions for the main locations of interest to walkers who may wish to split or combine more than one route. All will provide an excellent lunch so make a good walking destination.

MOUNTAIN HUTS, BERGHOTELS AND RESTAURANTS

This entire mountain region is surrounded by a wonderful network of mountain huts, *berghotels* and restaurants, making good destinations for a walk or an overnight stay with the opportunity to link more than one route together over two or more days. A full list can be found in Appendix A, and these are shown on the route maps provided.

All mountain huts serve meals. Additionally, mountain restaurants are spread throughout the area and make good refreshment stops or destinations in themselves. Cable car stations also tend to have at least one restaurant or café, and other facilities.

Staying in a mountain hut

Visiting one or more mountain huts and, better still, spending a couple of nights up high, is a quintessential part of the Swiss mountain walking experience. For many it's a new experience, but it is easy to get the hang of it.

On arrival change into hut shoes, either the ones provided (usually crocs or similar) or ones you have brought yourself. Check in with the guardian or guardienne who manages the hut: they will allocate a bed/space in the dorm for you and your party. Blankets or duvets and pillows are provided in the dormitories, but you will need a sleeping bag liner – these can be rented in most huts, so check when you call to book; silk ones are lighter and more comfortable.

Do book well ahead – huts may be busy and staff need to plan meals in advance. Most hut staff speak some English, but it's a good opportunity to unleash your inner linguist. If your plans change, or if you are unable to get to the hut, call to let them know. Failing to arrive at a scheduled hut may lead to a search being instigated if you are thought to have gone missing.

Meals are taken communally, and the guardian will allocate seating. Dinner is generally at 18:00 or 19:00 but check on arrival. Meals vary but will often start with soup, followed by salad, main course and a simple dessert. You will be asked about your breakfast time – for walkers normally between 06:00 and 07:00. Settle your bill either after dinner or in the morning. Before you depart, leave your bed space tidy, folding all blankets and other bedding, and check you have got all your kit.

Sleeping is usually either in 4–8 person rooms or in larger dorms. Most huts have recently installed additional screening for privacy and hygiene. Bedtime is generally before 22:00, when the hut goes quiet and the late-night rustling of plastic bags is to be avoided. Huts also serve climbers, who may slip out any time after 02:00 depending on their route. Sort your bed out early, keep your gear tucked away and tidy, get washing and personal tasks out of the way and then settle back to enjoy the late afternoon and evening. Take in the views, the sunsets and sunrises and enjoy the chance to make new friends, new memories and new plans.

OTHER LOCAL FACILITIES

All the larger villages have a range of shops, cafes and restaurants, and most have at least one bank with a cashpoint. There are Co-op supermarkets near the main station in Grindelwald, and in Wengen and Mürren. Other food shops can be found elsewhere in Grindelwald and in the other villages. There are outdoor stores in Grindelwald, Lauterbrunnen, Wengen and Mürren, as well as other sports shops and wellness services.

There are hospitals in Interlaken and Meiringen. Grindelwald, Lauterbrunnen, Wengen and Mürren all have pharmacies and doctors.

MAPS

Swiss mapping is excellent and clear. However, it is crucial you buy a Wanderkarte, a map marked with the footpath network – versions without the paths highlighted may be things of beauty, but they are difficult to use for walking.

Recommended maps are as follows:

- **Swisstopo 3323T Jungfrau Region at 1:33,000 1km = 3cm** is essentially a blown-up 1:50,000 scale covering between Grosse Scheidegg in the east to Kandersteg in the west, including the Faulhorn and surrounding mountains. Light and waterproof.
- **Swisstopo 254T Interlaken at 1:50,000, 1km = 2cm** comprises high-quality relief-shaded mapping of the entire area including Interlaken and the two lakes on waterproof paper, with walking routes clearly marked, but the scale is perhaps less good for walking.
- **Kümmerly + Frey Jungfrau Region sheet 18 at 1:60,000, 1km = 2.5cm** covers the whole area. Water resistant.
- **Kompass also publish a waterproof Jungfrau Region 84 map at 1:40,000**, which clearly shows the landscape and paths in a slightly different style.
- Routes in the higher part of the Lauterbrunnen valley (Untersteinberg, Obersteinberg) are just off the recommended

1:33,000 Swisstopo map but a good map is included on the **Hinteres Lauterbrunnen leaflet** available at Tourist Information Centres and accommodation around Stechelberg.

Map sources are given in Appendix A.

The route maps provided in this guidebook are at 1:50,000, 1km = 2cm, unless stated otherwise. These are derived from open-source data but have been reviewed in detail by the authors. Spellings and heights have been standardised as far as possible against Swisstopo mapping, but be aware that different maps and digital data have a range of heights and that signpost heights and spellings may differ slightly from those on the maps.

GPX TRACKS

GPX tracks for the routes in this guidebook are available to download free at www.cicerone.co.uk/1114/GPX. A GPS device is an excellent aid to navigation, but you should always carry a map and compass and know how to use them. GPX files are provided in good faith, and are accurate for the general purpose for which they have been recorded – mountain walking following marked paths. If following GPX tracks you should always consider their accuracy, especially taking into consideration the steep terrain,

Many houses have wonderful displays of flowers

The Tissot cliff walk at First

always assess likely danger areas and take due care in any situation you find yourself in.

APPS

In our digital world, apps are a valuable component of the walker's toolkit. The area is covered by many digital mapping resources, such as Outdoor Active and PhoneMaps. The following apps are specifically recommended for the walking visitor.

Mapping – Swisstopo provides access to all the Swiss mapping databases, in online and offline (downloadable) formats. Different tiles can be selected and bought, but it is important to download the footpath layer. The maps are available in several apps, Swisstopo itself and Swiss Mobility are just two.

Travel – SBB is a complete Swiss travel app for trains, buses and connecting cable cars, as well as some other services. The app brings together the entirety of the Swiss public transport system into a seamless whole. It's easy to use, linking with online payments and storing a Swiss Pass if you have applied for this as well. Note that if you have any type of discount card, you will need to show a printout (even if you have an e-ticket) when tickets are inspected.

Weather – MeteoSchweiz/ MeteoSuisse is a weather app from the Swiss meteorological agency that has full forecasting capabilities. It takes a little time to get the hang of, as it has lots of resources to explore, but it's worth the effort and is a bit more accurate than more general weather apps that don't fully account for Swiss mountain conditions.

Resort Information – the Jungfrau app is free to download and contains detailed information about the facilities in the region.

PREPARATION

It is much better to be fit before starting a Swiss mountain walking holiday. If you are hill fit for your home country, you should have few or no issues. Even a few lower walks will help with your preparation, especially if you manage two or three days together in walking boots and carrying a rucksack; it should assist in your acclimatisation to the higher altitude. At 1600m and 1800m you may feel little effect, but over 2500m the effect of the altitude will kick in, and you should gain height progressively before going far above 3000m. If you develop a headache, the best thing to do is to descend.

EQUIPMENT

For all except a few routes in this book, no special equipment beyond regular hiking gear is needed. You shouldn't need an ice axe and crampons on most of these routes, certainly after mid-July. However, crampons or micro-spikes might be needed for shaded north-facing routes in early summer or after recent snowfall.

If you plan to tackle harder routes in early summer, an ice axe and crampons could be a useful addition, assuming you have the necessary mountaineering experience to use them. Via ferrata protection (harness, lanyard, helmet) is not required for any of the routes described in this book.

Good footwear comes first. Boots are recommended: light- to mid-weight is ideal, but many walkers are happy using trainers or approach shoes. Use what you would generally use on a rocky hike.

Good waterproofs are next. You may see no rain whatsoever for the whole of a two-week holiday, but mountain weather is changeable, so you could experience rain daily. Late-afternoon thunderstorms are likely to be the main issue, so the best plan is to finish the day in good time; a thunderstorm can make you wet and cold very quickly. A modern, light- to mid-weight jacket and waterproof trousers are quite adequate for these routes in summer.

You will also need a suitable rucksack to carry your waterproofs, food for the day, spare fleece, hat, gloves, first-aid kit, water, camera, etc. A 20–30 litre rucksack is ample. Warm clothing and boots are recommended for walking on the glacier between Jungfraujoch and the Mönchsjochhütte.

USING THIS GUIDE

This guide provides 50 walking routes split between Grindelwald, Wengen, the Lauterbrunnen valley and Mürren, with through routes from Meiringen in the east, and to Griesalp in the west.

Distance, walking time, ascent and descent for each route are shown, together with a broad grade or indication of difficulty. Access is outlined and the main refreshment opportunities are mentioned.

Walking times

The walking times in this guide will usually closely match the signposted times on the yellow signs throughout the region. They are based on the steady pace of a reasonably fit hill/ mountain walker and don't allow for stops, lunch, afternoon cake, long siestas or photo sessions, so in practice you will need to adjust these timings to match your own preferences. A five-hour walking day with several

long stops might result in seven to eight hours on the mountain.

You should also consider your fitness and acclimatisation. Even if you are fit, take time to get used to the altitude. If you are flying in from abroad, bear in mind that the combined effect of jet lag and altitude can be challenging, throwing all walking times into disarray, so do make allowances in the first few days of a trip and start with some easier routes. In most cases, times that were challenging at the start of a holiday will seem much easier after a few days.

Grades

Swiss paths are graded into three levels of path:

Hiking trails (*wanderweg, chemins pédestres*) don't place any particular demands on the walker.

Red/white paint splashes indicate mountain paths

Gradings used in this guide	
Grade 1	An easy walk, mainly on undemanding, yellow paths or tracks, but likely with some red-and-white sections, in the valley or just above.
Grade 2	A moderate walk on clear and mainly straightforward mountain paths. No significant exposure or problematic ground on the route; however, the route may still be long, with considerable up and down and an occasional rail or steps.
Grade 3	A harder mountain walk on higher red-and-white mountain paths. Ascents, descents and walk times will be long, and in places there may be trickier ground, exposure and aided sections (cables, steps, ladders). Situated further away from valley bases and habitation.
Grade 4	A high, hard mountain walk, usually taking in parts of blue alpine trails. Considerable ascent and descent will be involved, the ground will be rough and rocky, there may be exposed passages and there will probably be aided sections with cables, steps and ladders. These may include straightforward glacier crossings.

They are marked on the ground in yellow or with yellow diamonds (not to be confused with the signposts, which are also yellow).

Mountain hiking trails (*bergwanderwege, itinéraire de montagne*) require walkers to be sure-footed, unafraid of heights, physically fit and experienced in the mountains. They are signposted with red-and-white waymarks or pointers on the yellow signposts.

Alpine trails (*alpine wanderwege, chemins de randonnée alpine*) demand that users are sure-footed, unafraid of heights and physically very fit; alpine experience and additional mountain equipment may be required. The paths are marked with blue-and-white waymarks or blue signs.

Most paths are well graded. Yellow paths are easy; blue paths are hard. Red-and-white paths, the mountain hiking trails, cover a wide range of walking, so we have provided a more nuanced grading structure (see table).

Bear in mind that a route is given a grade as a whole, so there may be an occasional harder section on a Grade 2 route, and a Grade 4 may have substantial sections of easier walking.

It's important to note that as snow and ice on mountain slopes melt, landslides can occur and paths can become damaged by subsidence from below or stonefall from above, so take account of path conditions as you find them and alter your plans accordingly.

SCHYNIGE PLATTE TO FIRST

The Schreckhorn seen clearly from the ridge above Spitzen (Walk 4)

WALK 1
Schynige Platte Panoramaweg

Start/Finish	Schynige Platte 1967m
Distance	5.5km
Total ascent	225m
Total descent	225m
Grade	2
Time	1hr 45min
Max altitude	2025m above Schynige Platte (2069m if Oberberghorn is included)
Refreshments	Schynige Platte
Access	Schynige Platte cog railway from Wilderswil

This walk is utterly fantastic on a fine clear day. Superb panoramic views are enjoyed throughout, and although the actual walking time is shown at under two hours, you will probably want to spend much more time, just to enjoy the views in all directions, and to take photographs. The walk is described anti-clockwise, but can be reversed. The superb views can be equally enjoyed in either direction. The Alpine Garden at Schynige Platte is also worthwhile, and entrance is free.

Superb views of the mountains stretching from the Wetterhorn all the way through to beyond the Breithorn, and to the Schilthorn, provide numerous opportunities for photography, so take your time here.

Take the cog railway from Wilderswil which climbs 1400m steadily and steeply to **Schynige Platte** with views of the valley below and Breinzersee. The train takes 45min; allow 1hr 15min from Grindelwald.

On arriving at the top station, walk back along the platform towards the restaurant, cross the tracks and take the path downhill. After 0.3km keep on the main path. Descend gently, then fork left after 0.5km. The path now rises a little then continues along a balcony route as it weaves around the hillside towards the **Loucherhorn** (2231m), which rises in rocky towers ahead. ◄

On reaching a path junction after 3.3km at 1985m, go right if you wish to climb further, (with good views

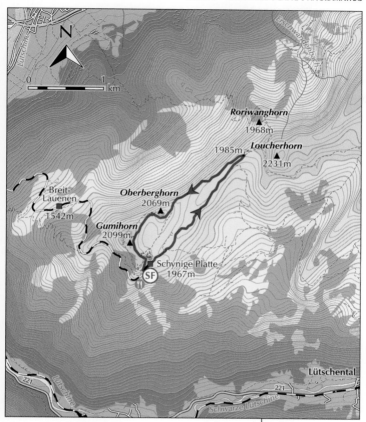

over the ridge just a short distance further on) otherwise turn sharp left, climb a metal staircase to reach the path which now takes a line along the cliff edge, with superb views down to Interlaken, the Thunersee and Brienzersee glistening far below, and a wall of mountains behind. Although the path keeps very close to the edge of the cliffs, there is no exposure to worry about.

Superb views east from the summit of the Oberberghorn to the Loucherhorn and mountains beyond and Brienzersee below

There are fine views from this modest peak. Allow an additional 20–30min for a round trip ascent.

After 3.75km (about 1hr) a path forks left leading directly to the station and Alpine Garden, otherwise take the right fork to continue climbing easily below cliffs around a bowl in the hillside, then after a further 15min, look for a path up to the **Oberberghorn** (2069m). ◄

If not climbing the Oberberghorn, keep left then fork left to descend a little, then climb to reach a level path leading round below the **Gumihorn** (2099m) to a view-point above the Alpine Garden and station. Descend the path in two zigzags to reach the Schynige Platte station.

The Alpine Garden is home to 730 alpine plants found above the tree line in their natural environment. The Alpine Garden is twinned with the Rokko Alpine Garden in the Japanese city of Kobe, and together, the two institutions exchange knowledge related to ecology, culture, tourism and education. The garden is open daily 8:30–5:45pm. +41 (0)33 828 73 76 alpengarten.ch.

WALK 2
Schynige Platte – Faulhorn – First

Start	Schynige Platte 1967m
Finish	First 2165m
Distance	16km
Total ascent	950m
Total descent	750m
Grade	3
Time	5hr 30min
Max altitude	2681m on the Faulhorn
Refreshments	Schynige Platte, Berghaus Männdlenen, Hotel Faulhorn, First
Access	Schynige Platte is reached by the train from Wilderswil

This is one of the great walks of the region high along the ridge above the Brienzersee with almost continual views of the Oberland mountain wall to the south. From the start the views cover the Lauterbrunnen valley and surrounding peaks, then the Jungfrau and its neighbours and finally the Wetterhorn. With two mountain restaurants, supplies are no problem. The route is continually above 2000m and will take most of a day. The path is well-marked and clear, but the section between Berghaus Männdlenen and the Faulhorn could become a challenge in poor visibility.

Take the train from Wilderswil to **Schynige Platte**. The old cog railway climbs slowly for 1400m in around 45min with occasional views through the forest to the lakes far below. ▶

Cross the railway tracks and descend slightly. The route is clearly signed, initially on a broad track. Descend into an attractive ablation valley, surrounded by the limestone towers of the Oberberghorn (2069m). The path keeps right with views across to the Jungfrau, before it climbs gradually to a **path junction** at 2029m, 45min.

At the station there is an Alpine Garden, hotel and restaurant as well as the gentle Panoramic Trail described in Walk 1.

The ground here is rockier, and the limestone pavements will continue well past the Berghaus Männdlenen.

Keep right here. A 10m climb here to a lip looks down over the lakes below. The path skirts under the Loucherhorn on a path signed Loucherhorn Grätli. This gives a good view back to the start and the mountains above Mürren and Lauterbrunnen. The path turns left on a broad saddle and becomes wider, then passes another shoulder of the **Loucherhorn**. ◄

After a short climb to **Egg** (2066m), keep to the right as the path gradually ascends the flanks of another limestone tower, the **Indri-Sägissa** (2462m), with views to the peaceful Sägistalsee below, with the dramatic bulky peak of the Schwabhoren ahead, its strata exposed by glacial forces. Climb steadily to a corner (**Gotthard**, 2276m) and

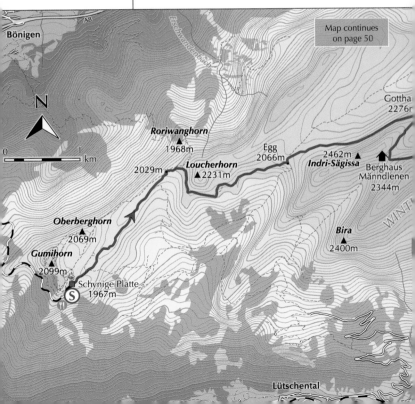

Map continues on page 50

Bönigen

N

0   1 km

Gottha
2276r

Roriwanghorn
1968m

Egg
2066m

2462m ▲
Indri-Sägissa

Berghaus
Männdlenen
2344m

Loucherhorn
▲2231m

2029m

Oberberghorn
2069m

Gumihorn
2099m

Schynige Platte
(S) 1967m

Bira
2400m

WINT

Lütschental

then climb to the **Berghaus Männdlenen** (2344m, 2hr 45min).

The **Berghaus Männdlenen**, formerly known as the Weber Hut, sits on a saddle with north and south views. It provides meals and has accommodation for 30. It's likely that you will arrive around lunchtime so it's a good place for a break.

The path climbs steeply above the *Berghaus* with a short (but not difficult) chained section to reach the Winteregg ridge. Continue with brief climbs and occasional short descents passing a large cairn and a few marker posts. ▸

A path heads left but keep right for the Faulhorn, now clearly visible ahead. At 2567m, there is a choice, either directly up the steep west ridge (the sign says *Abkürzung*

The trail weaves around substantial limestone outcrops after the traverse round the Loucherhorn

This section could be a challenge in poor visibility, but the path is waymarked and clear.

Gratweg – ridge shortcut) or take the traversing path and climb the broader and easier east ridge taking only a few minutes longer. Take the longer way if you are feeling any exposure. Whichever you choose, arrive at the **Faulhorn** with its hotel (2681m, 4hrs).

THE HOTEL FAULHORN

The Faulhorn is one of the oldest mountain inns in the Alps, dating from 1830, although improved and extended several times since then. There are 360° views across Switzerland to the Jura, but the mountain wall to the south dominates the views, especially in the glow of dawn and sunset. It's a great place to spend a night.

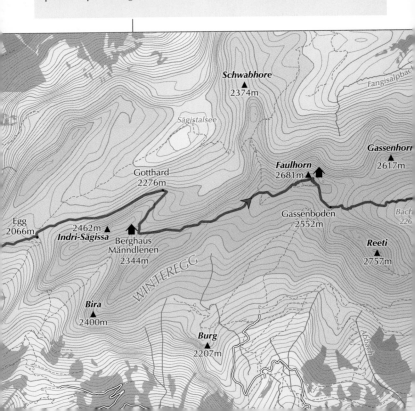

Take the wide path that descends the east ridge in easy zigzags. After 15min pass the **Gassenboden** saddle at 2552m, and keep on the main path left which drops, steeply at times, to the attractive **Bachsee (2265m)** around 45min from the Faulhorn. ▶

Pass the lakes and keep to the main wide and way-marked path for First. At one point the path climbs above a stony track, but the two merge 400m later. After a shelter (the **Gummihitta** at 2272m) continue, now descending. Look out for a right turn with the regular wanderweg marker which leads directly to First. You may want to finish on the cliff walk which edges alongside the cliffs directly to the restaurant, otherwise keep straight down for the **First gondola station** (2165, 5hr 30min).

The backdrop of Wetterhorn, Schrekhorn, Fiescherhorn and Finsteraarhorn is stunning. This descent could well take much longer than the walking time allowed, as your eyes are constantly drawn to the view.

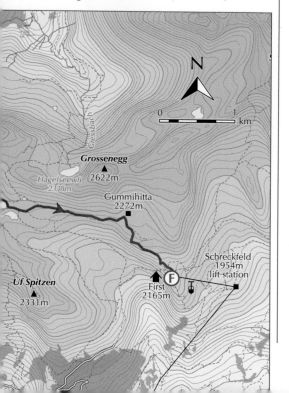

WALK 3
First – Bachsee – Faulhorn – Bussalp

Start	First 2165m
Finish	Bussalp 1796m
Distance	10.5km
Total ascent	560m
Total descent	930m
Grade	2–3
Time	4hr
Max altitude	2681m at the summit of the Faulhorn
Refreshments	The Faulhorn hotel and restaurant at Bussalp
Access	From the First gondola station

This walk combines two of the region's most iconic places – Bachsee and the Faulhorn – and descends a quiet valley to an alp hamlet high above Grindelwald, happily served by an hourly bus during the summer. The First lift gives access to a range of walks, and the 50min walk to the beautiful Bachsee is just the best-known of these. The Faulhorn Berghotel is a long-established mountain inn, perched atop its peak with 360° views including the whole mountain wall above Grindelwald.

Having taken in the view from **First**, take the path leading away from the cable car station, with signs to many destinations including Faulhorn with a suggested time of 2hr 20min, and Bachsee. Pass above the cliff walkway which looks high and exposed, but safe. The path climbs steadily, it is very well built. Indeed, there seems little reason why the lake cannot be reached in flip-flops and possibly the Faulhorn too.

The path climbs steadily through mountain pastures.

Views ahead stretch to the Faulhorn hotel and summit 500m above whilst behind it's hard to decide whether the Wetterhorn, Schrekhorn, Finsteraarhorn, Fiescherhorn or Eiger (seen here from the east) is the more appealing summit.

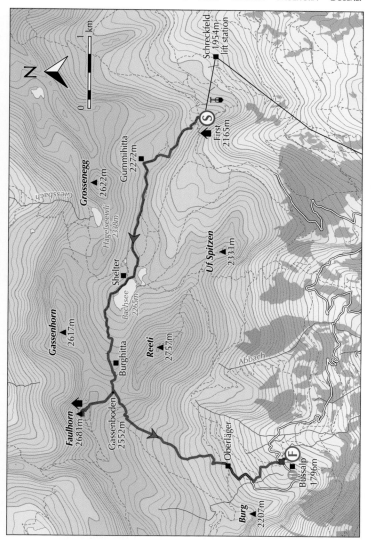

The peaceful Bachsee is a mecca for walkers and all visitors

The main lake is a substantial photogenic tarn understandably much loved by picnickers, with the best views and photos from the far end of the main lake.

Pass the **Gummihitta** (one of several shelters in case of need on this popular route) at 2272m and soon after (based on the current routing of the path) take a path that climbs above the track, rejoining in 400m. The path levels out and arrives at the two **Bachsee lakes** (2265m, 50min), and another shelter and even a summer toilet. ◄

Signs suggest the Faulhorn is 1hr 20min further, which may be a generous estimate. Follow the path around the lake to the far end and begin climbing on the well-maintained track, passing the **Burgihitta** (shelter) before emerging on the **Gassenboden** saddle at 2552m. From here it's a stiff 20min to the summit of the **Faulhorn** (2681m, 2hr 15min).

Building at the **Faulhorn** started in 1830, making it one of the oldest *berghotels* in the alps. It has been extended and modernised since then and makes both a great destination for a day walk or an overnight stop, when the views in all directions, with sunrise and sunset on the Oberland mountains making for a special experience.

Having taken in the undoubtedly spectacular views down to the Brienzersee and south to the mountain wall, explored the summit area and taken refreshments, descend the way you came, back to the **Gassenboden** saddle in 15min.

▸ This route turns right here and takes a good path gradually descending. The descent is signed as taking 1hr 15min, in practice it is likely to take longer, and we have allowed 1hr 45min from the summit.

It is quite possible to descend directly to First and its gondola system in around 1hr 30min (perhaps to try the cliff walkway).

Initially, this weaves through rocky areas but soon starts to descend more steeply on easier ground. At 2050m pass the first summer farm (**Oberläger**), and look at the scene of summer pastures, cows grazing calmly but noisily, and tiny summer farms in the mountain bowl above Bussalp. Join a paved farm road and continue down to the right but be alert for the poorly signed path that heads left from the road. Follow this (or the road in 15–20min longer) directly down to **Bussalp** (1796m, 4hr), with its hourly bus and welcoming restaurant.

WALK 4
First – Spitzen – Bussalp – the Höhenweg 2200

Start	First 2165m
Finish	Bussalp 1796m
Distance	8.75km
Total ascent	310m
Total descent	680m
Grade	2
Time	3hr
Max altitude	2401m at Fernandeshütta
Refreshments	First, Bussalp
Access	First gondola lift, bus from Bussalp

This is a great walk for a good clear day, having all the ingredients you could wish for to make the route really interesting, and rewarding. The first part of the walk is along the easy track rising to the beautiful and much-visited Bachsee, with great photo opportunities if the water is still. From the lake the path climbs easily to Spitzen on the Hireleni ridge, then hugs the cliff edge climbing to a highpoint at around 2400m – with superb views. The descent path into the next valley passes easily through a chaotic boulder field, then eases more steadily across pasture then down the hillside to reach Bussalp.

This walk can be combined with Walk 5 at the path junction at 2180m to make a much longer circular route back to First, or as far as the Waldspitz restaurant for a bus to Grindelwald.

Arriving at the **First** gondola station, take the broad track in the signed direction of Bachsee. This will be the way most people will be going! The route rises steadily, passing a chalet and on past a small shelter (**Gummihitta**), then becomes more level for a while. After 3.4km there is a path off to the right (signed to Axalp) but ignore this and continue ahead on the track to arrive at **Bachsee** (2265m, 50min).

The two lakes at **Bachsee** are a popular spot, and you will not be alone here. To achieve the 'classic view' photograph, walk a little further around Bachsee on the level path to a grassy promontory. If you are lucky the water will be still, and the Schreckhorn and Finsteraarhorn will be perfectly mirrored in the Bachsee waters.

To continue on the walk, take the path between the two lakes, cross on a small bridge over the outflow from the higher lake and turn left. At a fork in the paths fork right on the higher path and climb steadily round a shoulder and descend slightly into a small valley with several small tarns to reach a path junction at **Spitzen** (2427m, 1hr 15min).

Turn right and continue climbing along the ridge line now with more fine views (and an airy drop) to the south.

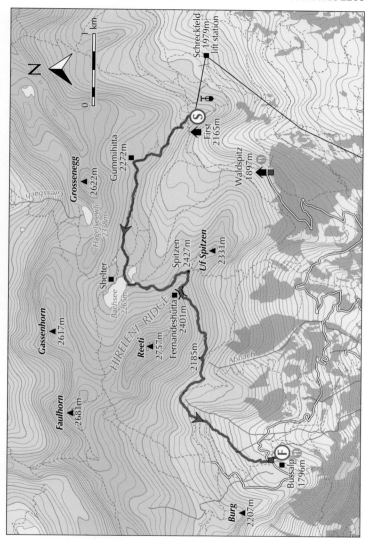

Superb panoramas at the Fernandeshütta

The path is good despite its airy location, and there is only a sense of the cliff to the left if you go off the path and peer over. After around 10min climbing arrive at a col and small wooden shelter **Fernandeshütta** (2401m, 1hr 30min).

> This is a great location to stop to take in the views, gather your breath and maybe have a picnic. Above is **Reeti** (2757m), the highest point on the ridge.

Descend carefully. The path threads through a large chaotic boulder field, but red and white paint splashes clearly show the way and there is nothing difficult. Eventually the path escapes the boulders then rises slightly to a point by an isolated large boulder where the way down is now clearly seen on a gently descending path across the hillside to reach a path junction 2185m, 2hr 15min.

The path left provides an opportunity to return to **First**, via **Waldspitz**, and makes for an interesting circular walk. (See Walk 5)

For Bussalp, continue ahead, and after 200 metres, cross a shoulder with the Feld alp buildings below, and the cluster of chalets at Oberlager seen across the hillside ahead. Traverse the pastures on an undulating path, drop down to cross a stream (the stream gully is usually filled with snow) then continue down. Turn left onto the path signed Bussalp and the Hohenweg 2200. Cross straight over a track, climb over a two-step ladder over a wall, and continue down to reach **Bussalp** (1796m, 8.75km, 3hr).

WALK 5
Bussalp – Waldspitz – First – the Höhenweg 2000

Start	Bussalp 1796m
Finish	First 2165m
Distance	12km
Total ascent	790m
Total descent	420m
Grade	2
Time	4hr 30min
Max altitude	2187m at path junction above Feld
Refreshments	Bussalp, Waldspitz, First
Access	Bus to Bussalp, and First gondola to Grindelwald, or bus from Waldspitz
Warning	Although most of the route is grade 2, the final climb to First is a steep, well-maintained but exposed mountain path

This walk is described in an easterly direction, taking advantage of the superb views throughout the walk of the mountain wall stretching from the Wetterhorn all the way through to the Breithorn in the far west. There are options to combine with either the Bort to Bussalp route (Walk 6) or more logically, with the higher First to Bussalp route (Walk 4), where the two walks meet at the highpoint path junction just to the east of Feld. Traverse pastures with superb views and a natural 'rock garden' threading through boulders and rocks on a grassy path. Beautiful woods full of alpenrose reward at the end of the climb to Waldspitz (refreshments, bus stop), and the route finishes with the final climb to First on an exposed but well-made steep path.

From the bus stop walk down the road to the second turning on the left, taking the grassy path rising immediately after the turn (a red and white paint splash on a rock shows the way). Follow this good path as it traverses and climbs the hillside, mainly at a steady gradient, over a low stone wall and straight across a track, eventually meeting a path junction 45min. Turn right and continue up, cross a gully on a metal bridge, (snow collects here all year round) to reach a grassy bowl then climb to a small saddle overlooking the alp farm buildings above **Feld** (1hr 15min).

Climb gently to a path junction at 2185m and take the right fork signed to Waldspitz and First. (The path to the left leads to Fernandeshütta and Spitzen on the Hohenweg 2200 – see Walk 4). Contour round the hillside and descend to an isolated chalet, then descend more steeply through a delightful area of boulders and rocks, a natural rock garden with grasses and flowers and superb views towards the Wetterhorn. Arrive at a path junction a little above **Spillmatten** (1hr 50min) and turn right.

Now on a grassy track, follow signs downhill to the lowest point of the walk. At first the continuing track is fairly level, but then the way ahead is straight and steep, then eases a little. Pass through a gate then take the signed path left up through woods ablaze with carpets

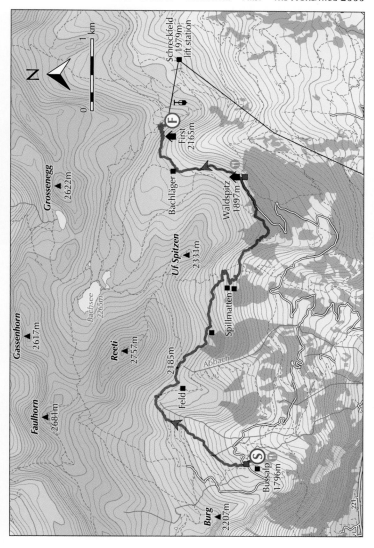

Approaching the final climb to First from Bachläger, with the Wetterhorn behind

of alpenrose in early summer. On reaching a track climb easily to **Waldspitz** (1897m, 3hr 30min, restaurant, bus stop).

> The **Waldspitz** is a popular location for weekend walkers and locals alike, enjoying fine views of the Eiger, Schreckhorn and Wetterhorn. There are options to eat inside or on the extensive terrace, and good basic accommodation is also available. With road access, the walk can be finished here with a bus back down to Grindelwald. www. gasthaus-waldspitz.ch.

Watch out for mountain bikers making a fast descent while you are on the track to Bachläger.

Now on the Höhenweg 2000, continue up the gravel track to a group of chalets and farm buildings at **Bachläger** and take the path right, now heading directly towards First. ◄

The path is made up of huge flat stones and rises easily, then begin the final ascent up steep zigzags which might feel a bit exposed, but the path is good and there is never a need to grasp onto things with your hands!

People on the First Cliff Walkway will be clearly seen just above. Finally, arrive at a saddle where you are suddenly surrounded by sightseers, walkers and mountain bikers. The cliff walkway is worthwhile and brings you directly to a viewing terrace and restaurant at **First** (2165m, 4hr 30min).

WALK 6
Bort to Bussalp – the Höhenweg 1600

Start	Bort gondola station 1561m
Finish	Bussalp 1796m
Distance	7.5km
Total ascent	390m
Total descent	155m
Grade	1
Time	2hr 15min
Max altitude	1797m Bussalp
Refreshments	Bort, Rasthysi, Bussalp
Access	First gondola from Grindelwald, return by bus from Bussalp
Note	This walk can be combined with Walk 7 to finish back in Grindelwald

This is an easy walk almost entirely on tracks and minor roads through the wooded hillsides and open pastures above Grindelwald. Although it involves some ascent, there is nothing steep, and there are fine views across the valley south and east to the mountains dominating the views – especially the Wetterhorn and Eiger, and to Kleine Scheidegg and Männlichen to the south. There are several places to stop for refreshments, and various points from which to take the bus down to Grindelwald if needed.

If the walk described is done in reverse, then there is less ascent involved, and the massive walls of the Wetterhorn and Mättenberg will be more constantly in view.

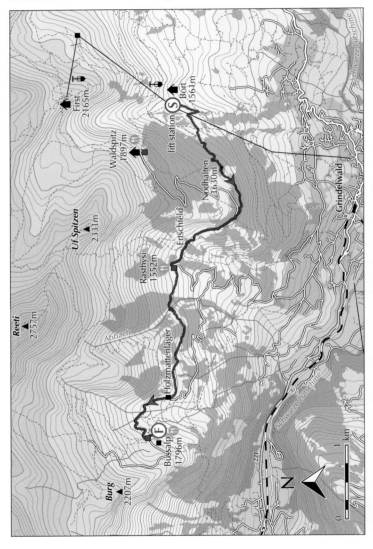

From the **Bort** gondola station, find the signed paths next to the Alpine Hotel Bort. Take the path down with the playground on the right, and after 0.3km turn sharp right signed to Nodhalten. Pass under the cables, over a stream and cross pastures up to Ertschfeld (1540m). Continue up ahead, ignoring the track joining on the right.

Follow the gravel track climbing steadily through woods with tall pine trees, and when the track levels off keep left signed Bussalp. There are fine views of the Wetterhorn and along the mountain range including the Eiger, and soon reach the chalet at **Nodhalten**, (1630m, 30min). After a further 10min meet a quiet narrow road and continue ahead (left) to Holewang, a small cluster of farm buildings and chalets 1578m, 1hr, and then round the next corner find the chalet at **Rasthysi** (1552m, refreshments, bus stop).

Easy woodland walking on the way to Rasthysi

Fork right up the gravel track, which climbs steadily. At a fork after a further 30min keep right to continue to climb on a track (signed to Bussalp and Mittelläger). Arriving at a road at **Holzmattenläger** continue up the road to **Bussalp** (1796m, 2hr 15min).

Bussalp enjoys superb views down into the valley, and across to the great wall of mountains including the Wetterhorn and Eiger. The highest point on one of the bus routes from Grindelwald, Bussalp is a good starting point or end point for the three main Höhenweg routes across the hillside above Grindelwald. There is a restaurant, terrace and accommodation.

WALK 7
Bussalp to Grindelwald

Start	Bussalp 1796m
Finish	Grindelwald 1040m
Distance	6km
Total ascent	15m
Total descent	770m
Grade	1
Time	1hr 45min
Max altitude	1796m
Refreshments	Bussalp
Access	Bus from Grindelwald, or link with Walks 3, 4 or 6

Many of the walks around the hillsides above Grindelwald begin or end at Bussalp. This walk is an easy downhill route almost entirely on tracks and minor roads through woods and open pastures, passing the elegant Abbach waterfall on the route. There are fine and constant views across the valley to the main high mountains and to Kleine Scheidegg and Männlichen. There are various options on the way to take the bus down to Grindelwald if needed.

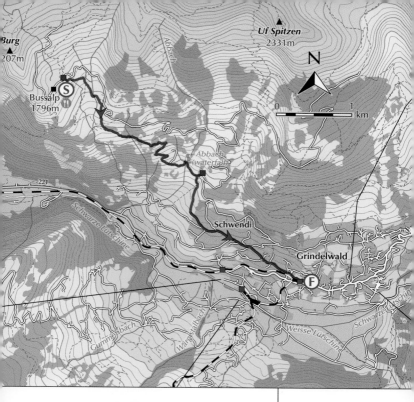

From the bus stop at **Bussalp** walk down the road for just a few metres and immediately take the descending path on the right, following yellow posts and signs across meadows. Cross a stream and take the path slightly right in front of the farm buildings signed to Grindelwald.

Descend through more meadows, with the Eiger dominating the view ahead, and cross straight over a track, then meet the track again. Continue downhill, following yellow footpath signs all the way. The gravel track becomes a small road, and continue down in broad zig-zags to reach the **Abbach waterfall** after 1hr 10min.

Cowbells hang outside a farm building at Bussalp

The **Abbach waterfall** is a slender fall as the water from the river Abbach drops in two stages over about 50m into a small pool.

Continue down the road shortly arriving at a small building (bus stop). Take the descending grassy path down to the right signed to Grindelwald, following this steadily down between meadows to meet a road and the first houses of **Schwendi**. Keep following the yellow path signs along the road steadily downhill in a south-easterly direction directly to the train station at **Grindelwald** (6km, 1hr 45min).

WALK 8

Bort – Alpenvogelpark – Hotel Wetterhorn

Start	Bort 1561m
Finish	Hotel Wetterhorn, (Oberer Gletscher) 1228m
Distance	6km
Total ascent	180m
Total descent	510m
Grade	1–2
Time	1hr 45min
Max altitude	1646m at path junction above Bort
Refreshments	Bort and Hotel Wetterhorn
Access	First gondola lift from Grindelwald, bus from various points on the Grosse Scheidegg to Grindelwald road

This walk is an interesting mid-level walk, and a continuation of the Höhenweg 1600 described in Walk 6 between Bort and Bussalp. It's true to its name too, as the route tends to be always hovering around the 1500m–1600m height as it traverses the hillside passing less-visited alpine meadows and streams and with constant views towards the Wetterhorn. The Alpenvogelpark is a small alpine bird park, and you can end the walk here, or continue across meadows then down to Hotel Wetterhorn for well-earned refreshments. Then either walk down to Grindelwald (see Walk 9) or take the bus the rest of the way.

Pass under the gondola station then take the ascending paved path to a path junction next to a stream. High above a steep path climbs to Waldspitz, but the Höhenweg route turns right and continues climbing a little more to a high point.

A track can be seen looping back downhill towards the Bort gondola station, but the way ahead takes the grassy path rising easily, with great views to both Grosse and Kleine Scheidegg and the huge wall of mountains between.

The Milibach stream and path junction above Bort

You will begin to hear the cascading water of the Bärgelbach stream, which cuts a deep trough into the soft shales of the hillside.

Descend steeply for 50m, then join an undulating gravel track across meadows dotted with chalets and barns then turn right onto a metalled road and immediately left to take another path, signed to Im underen Loichbiel (the signage reads Unterer Lauchbühl, Hohenweg 1600) at 2km, 30min.

Descend to **Bedeli**, then turn left climbing again on a gravel track. (The track to the right will take you down easily to Moos and Grindelwald.) ◄

Cross over the Bärgelbach on the bridge and climb back out of the streambed to 1550m where you keep right to join a track and gently pass though pine woods and across meadows then down to **Im underen Loichbiel** 1hr 15min (bus stop).

Turn right and walk down the road for 500 metres to reach the **Alpenvogelpark** located on a sharp hairpin bend (bus stop). Now take the path left by the restaurant

which traverses directly across meadows for 300 metres
to reach a path junction at the same height of 1400m.
Turn right downhill, and on meeting the road continue
ahead past a small lake and picnic area to arrive at **Hotel
Wetterhorn** (Oberer Gletscher, 6km, 1hr 45min).

The **Alpenvogelpark** is a free facility funded entirely
by donations. The bird park features ravens, buz-
zards, mountain cock, and various owls – little owl,
eagle owl, tawny owl, barn owl and snowy owls.
www.alpenvogelpark.ch.

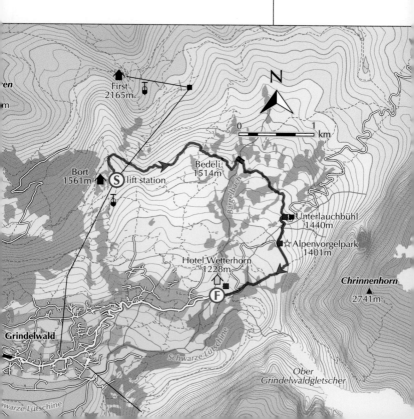

WALK 9

First – Grosse Scheidegg – Hotel Wetterhorn – Grindelwald

Start	First 2165m
Finish	Grindelwald 1040m
Distance	14km
Total ascent	120m
Total descent	1240m
Grade	1–2
Time	3hr 45min
Max altitude	2165m First gondola station
Refreshments	First, Grosse Scheidegg, Hotel Wetterhorn, restaurant above Am Stutz
Access	First gondola lift

This route has virtually no climbing with constant and magnificent views of the great mountain wall of Wetterhorn, Schreckhorn and Eiger, the distant Kleine Scheidegg and Männlichen rising ahead, with Grindelwald nestling in the valley below. An easy balcony walk from First meanders mainly downhill among meadows traversing the hillside, with fine views. From Grosse Scheidegg the route mainly follows closely to the sinuous road, crossing and re-crossing where the road makes hairpin turns, with some short sections in pine woods, particularly below Hotel Wetterhorn. The bus to Grindelwald can be accessed at various points on the route, to save tired legs, or to split the route into shorter sections.

From the gondola terminus at **First**, find a descending path signed to Grosse Scheidegg which passes in front of the Genepi Hütte, descending on steps to meet a wider gravel track. Continue down until the track makes a sharp right bend (at 2080m), then continue ahead now on a path ascending slightly, and after 100 metres fork right signed Grosse Scheidegg.

From First, pass the Genepi Hütte to briefly follow a track

The path gently descends hugging the hillside and where a path joins from the left just above **Grindel Oberläger**, continue ahead passing just above the chalets. ▶

Climb a little now and contour round the hillside, cross the Schafgraben stream then descend again and join the main track by a small wooden shelter. Follow this track descending round the hillside to **Grosse Scheidegg** (1962m, 1hr 25min).

From the summit of Grosse Scheidegg, take the small path opposite the berghotel signed for the Via Alpina 1 and to Hotel Wetterhorn and Grindelwald.

Cross straight over the road and continue down. Cross over the road at a chalet at Blaserie, then cross again a few minutes later. A little further downhill, cross the road again, cutting off a hairpin, walk down the road for 180 metres then turn right onto the path just at the apex of the bend in the road.

Descend on a pretty section between boulders, touch the road at the next bend, then continue on the path now through pine woods. Touch and leave the road again,

The hillside is covered with bilberry and juniper, turning the whole area crimson and orange in late summer and autumn.

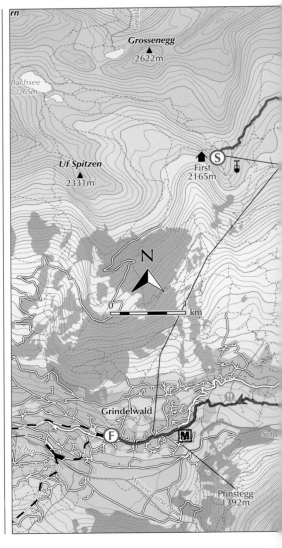

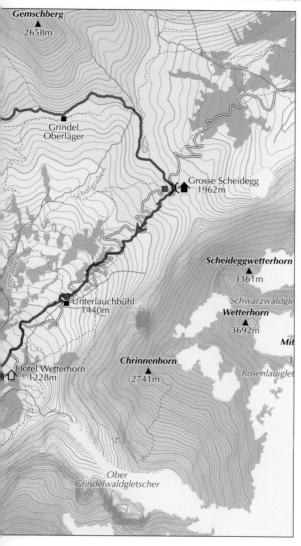

descending more steeply for a while, cross the road, cross pastures then cut across three successive hairpins to reach a path junction next to the road at **Unterlauchbühl** (1440m, 2hr 30min, bus stop).

Take the small track passing to the left of the Schwendibiel hostel and descend across meadows to Shiirli. Join the road and walk for 500 metres down it, then take the signed path descending to the right to arrive at **Hotel Wetterhorn** (1228m, 3hr).

> The location of Hotel Wetterhorn is also known as **Oberer Gletscher**. The hotel provides a welcoming spot, with good food served in the restaurant and outside. Good quality modern rooms are also available. www.wetterhorn-hotel.ch.

The continuing descending route begins at the far side of the car park opposite the hotel. Take the gravel track through pine woods steadily down, then follow the path right and continue down, cross the Bärgelbach stream, then climb to cross broad meadows dotted with wooden barns and reach a track and a bench under a tree. Turn left then immediately right and continue the descent. Cross the Horbach stream, climb to an isolated chalet then turn left down a small road, with a mountain restaurant seen up on the right. Now passing among more houses, follow signs all the way to Grindelwald, emerging by the Grindelwald Museum on the left.

> The **museum** is something of a find, and well worth the modest entry fee. Exhibits depict traditional rural life, mountaineering, skiing and tourism. Historical photographs and drawings show the extent of the glaciers in times past, as well as how the town itself has changed and developed. www.grindelwald-museum.ch.

Now continue down the main street to the centre of **Grindelwald** (3hr 45min).

WALK 10
First – Bachsee – Waldspitz

Start	First 2165m
Finish	Waldspitz 1897m
Distance	6.5km
Total ascent	150m
Total descent	420m
Grade	1–2
Time	2hr
Max altitude	2265m at Bachsee
Refreshments	First, Restaurant at Waldspitz
Access	From the First gondola station

Bachsee is one of the gems of the Bernese Oberland, famed for its views and, if fortunate, photos with reflections of the facing mountains. This short route takes in the lake and descends easily to a fine mountain restaurant and bus stop.

Access to First is by the gondola lift and descent from Waldspitz is by bus, although a return to the First lift system is possible. The walk opens many other route options and can be extended in numerous ways, by heading round and above Bachsee, by returning to First (up a very steep hillside) or by descending to Bort and taking the lift down.

From the **First** gondola station take the path headed up signed for the Bachsee Lake. The path climbs firmly at first, up to a viewpoint, climbs more and turns left and starts a traverse. You are highly unlikely to be alone here, Bachsee is an understandably popular objective and the onward path leads to the Faulhorn (see Walk 3), also a popular destination.

The route throughout is a broad maintained path able to cope with the wide range of walkers attracted to the Bachsee.

The gentle path from First to the Bachsee attracts many visitors.
The Wetterhorn across the valley dominates the view

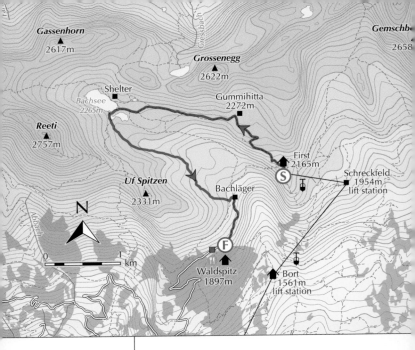

The path passes a shelter (**Gummihitta**, 2272m) then climbs briefly above the track to avoid a dip, descends again then continues undulating slightly until the lake appears (2265m, 50min).

There are two lakes at **Bachseealp**, a larger, higher one and smaller one below. Facing are the walls of the Wetterhorn, Schrekhorn, Finsteraarhorn, Fiescherhorn and to the right, the Eiger. The best photo spots are at the far end of the lake, reached in fewer than 10min, and in a calm early morning you may get a fine reflection of the peaks.

When you have absorbed the beauty and are ready to leave, start from the hut at the east end of upper lake. Pass by another hut and turn to cross a stream. Turn left downhill and keep left at the path junction and start the steady descent along a good path, this one signed as a mountain path. ▶ In early summer the alpenrose are bright red, and in autumn a blaze of orange. After 50min pass to the left of farm buildings below **Bachläger** and turn right on a track that descends in 10min to the restaurant and bus stop at **Waldspitz** (1897m, 2hr).

The bustle of the lakeside is quickly left behind, and with views ahead to First on its rocky outcrop as well as the mountains across the valley.

Options to extend or shorten the route

1   At Bachsee continue past the lake and climb towards the Faulhorn (See Walk 3).

2   At Waldspitz (or Bachläger) take the signed route back to First up the steep, exposed but well-made path (grade 2–3) in 1hr from Waldspitz. (See Walk 5).

3   By the bus stop at Waldspitz find the signed path that descends to Bort (1561m) in 40min to finish down the gondola.

4   To shorten the route, return to First from the Bachsee (45min).

The Waldspitz hotel and restaurant enjoys stunning views

WALK 11

The Schwarzhorn Circuit: First – Wart – Grosse Scheidegg

Start	First 2165m
Finish	Grosse Scheidegg 1962m
Distance	14.5km
Total ascent	800m
Total descent	1000m
Grade	3
Time	5hr
Max altitude	2705m at the Wart col between the Schwarzhorn and Wildgärst
Refreshments	First, then none until the end of the route at Grosse Scheidegg
Access	From the First gondola station

The Schwarzhorn lies high above First, with the Wetterhorn dominating the Grosse Scheidegg area, and is visible from almost all parts of the valley. Its circuit gives a remote mountain challenge in wild terrain. There are no Eiger views here, it is a very different experience. Most of the route is straightforward, and the remoteness and high mountain environment make it a worthy inclusion in this guide.

Check the times of the last buses from Grosse Scheidegg or gondola at First if you plan to return that way. The area 'behind' the Schwarzhorn faces north and can hold snow long into the summer and in the autumn, so check conditions before setting out. Under snow it is a much harder proposition.

From the gondola station, take the well-worn track signed for Bachsee, and in 40min, 10min before reaching the lake, find a **sign** (2276m) for Wildgärst.

Turn right here onto a much smaller path, much less used. You are now on the way less travelled. Pass a small tarn with possible reflections of the facing Reeti, and climb alongside rocks, coming to a path junction at

2517m, with options for the Faulhorn to the left, but keep right. The path starts to descend with the distant Wart col clearly seen.

Turning a corner on the descent to Grosse Scheidegg with views across the Rychenbachtal to the Engelhorner range

> We heard the **alpenhorn** long before we would see the player. He was clearly a master of his craft, and this was his chosen spot, just above the Hagelseewli lake, the backdrop of vast cliffs echoing and ampli-fying the notes. Lesley approached him, 'may I play?'. He happily agreed and Lesley made music in the mountains.

Pass another path junction (2361m) and keep straight on. There are attractive places to stop by the **Hagelseewli lake** (2338m, 1hr 20min). Cross the stream from the lake, and immediately climb a steep slope. This side is fine and grassy, but the descent on the far side is in almost perma-nent shade and may be snowy, icy, muddy, or all three, on outward sloping shale. But it's just a short section, a descent of 40m, and is soon over.

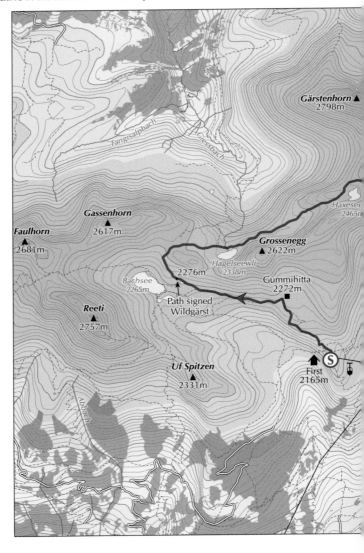

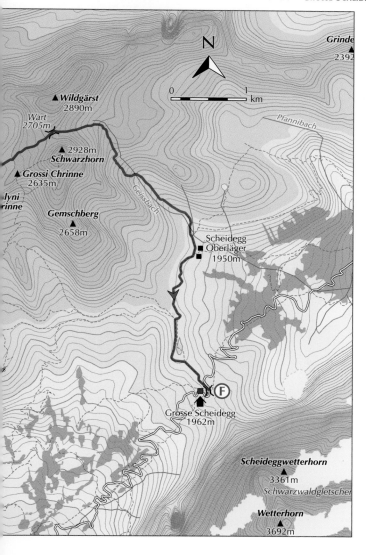

Enter a different world of glacier-levelled rocks. The Chlyni and Grossi Chrinne vertical cliffs loom on the right, the col seems distant ahead. It's a remote, wild setting. The route weaves around outcrops, trending upwards but with a few small descents. Keep an eye open for the red and white marks indicating the approximate route of the path. Pass the higher lake, the **Haxeseewli** (2465m), like its partner below, a magnificent setting.

Pass a path junction at 2590m (2hr 40min), where a via ferrata crosses the Grossi Chrinne and the routes meet here. Continue ahead, the col now less than 100m above and climb the increasingly rocky ground and likely a patch or two of snow before arriving at the **Wart col** (2705m, 3hr). ◀

Below and to the right see the remains of the tiny Blau Gletscherli, not long for this world, unfortunately.

Ascent of Wildgärst

The rounded dome of the Wildgärst (2890m) is above to the left. It's no match for the stern rocks of the Schwarzhorn it faces but its easily climbed in 30–40min, the round trip taking a little more than an hour with fine views in all directions.

Main route

To continue the route, head half-left from the col. Either cross and descend the seemingly ever-present snow or skirt it by keeping left. The direct route is usually good. Descend amongst rocky ribs; the path soon becomes easier before steepening on a good but steep and stony path tracing the course of the Geissbach stream.

After descending for 30min, come to a grassy and much friendlier descent through the valley of Wischbääch, arriving at a bridge and track at 1940m, before continuing to the farm buildings at **Scheidegg Oberläger** (1950m, 4hr 20min).

Climb gradually to Gratschärem with a possible return to First if you have time before the final cable car (1hr 20min trip). But keep on the track to **Grosse Scheidegg** (1962m, 5hr) and a well-earned refreshment opportunity.

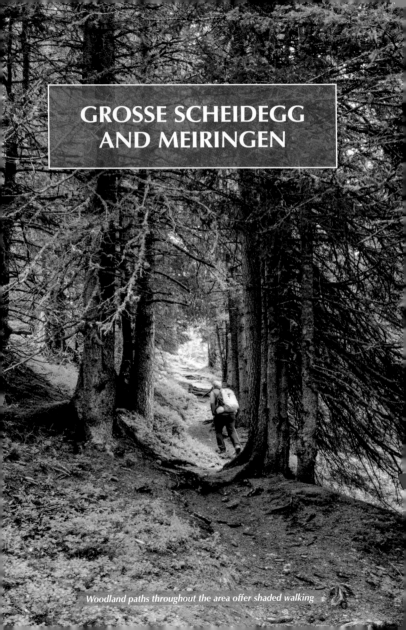

GROSSE SCHEIDEGG
AND MEIRINGEN

Woodland paths throughout the area offer shaded walking

WALK 12
Grosse Scheidegg to Schwarzwaldalp

Start	Grosse Scheidegg 1962m
Finish	Schwarzwaldalp 1455m
Distance	9km
Total ascent	90m
Total descent	600m
Grade	2
Time	2hr 30min
Max altitude	2007m Gratschärem
Refreshments	Grosse Scheidegg, Brochhütte and Schwarzwaldalp
Access	Bus from Grindelwald (and Meiringen) to Grosse Scheidegg
Note	Due to the nature of the fine glacial till on the hillside, the path can be muddy in places in wet weather. This route is best walked during dryer periods

This walk takes you into the northern hills below Grosse Scheidegg on an easy, mainly downhill route. Roughly divided into three sections, the first and final sections are on gravel tracks, providing good opportunities to admire the views without having to watch your feet all the time. The middle section is a delight, a mountain path gently traversing a hillside full of alpenrose and bilberries to a picnic area and shelter with fine views at Gibelplatti. A small but well-made path descends steeply with well-defined steps. There are excellent views throughout, mainly across the valley to (north to south) the Grosses Engelhorn, Gstellihorn, Wellhorn and Wetterhorn. Schwarzwaldalp has a hotel/restaurant with sun terrace and playground, as well as a fascinating old water-powered sawmill. (See Walk 13 for more information.)

Leaving **Grosse Scheidegg** on the track signed to First, after 1.3km of gentle climbing arrive at a path junction by a small shelter, **Gratschärem** 2006m, and take the track to the right.

Views down the Rychenbach valley from the Gibelplatti shelter and picnic area

Head down the track with the alp hamlet **Scheidegg Oberläger** ahead. Pass through the farm buildings and ignore the first turn right signed to Schwarzwaldalp, but continue round the corner to fork right at 1940m, cross the Geissbach stream and shortly after a sign indicates Schwarzwaldalp to the right at 1949m, with a steeper path rising to the left. The angle of the sign to Schwarzwaldalp is slightly confusing, essentially keep on the gravel track as it climbs steadily to 1981m, 1hr, when the path leaves the track to contour round the **Cheerhubel** (2213m).

This is a beautiful, almost level **path** and a real delight (unless very wet and muddy). Alpenrose covers the hillside, turning it a vibrant red in early summer, while in autumn the bilberry bushes provide wonderful colour of deep red and orange.

Views are across the Pfannibach valley and to the high mountains on the eastern side of the main valley.

After passing through some light woodland come to a small shelter, with a barbeque and bench seats. **Gibelplatti** (1947m, 1hr 20min). ◄ The path down is a small, steep but well-made path. Boards cover boggy areas, and the path then becomes grassy before meeting a track (2hr).

Turn right, cross the Pfannibach stream on a bridge, and keep on the track steadily in sweeping zigzags downhill, passing the popular **Brochhütte** at 1505m before the final descent to the road. Turn right to walk up the road to **Schwarzwaldalp**, 9km, 2hr 30min. Refreshments, picnic area, bus stop.

WALK 13
The Rychenbach valley: Schwarzwaldalp – Rosenlaui circuit

Start/Finish	Schwarzwaldalp 1455m
Distance	6.75km
Total ascent	170m
Total descent	170m
Grade	1
Time	2hr
Max altitude	1455m Schwarzwaldalp
Refreshments	Schwarzwaldalp, Hotel Rosenlaui
Access	Bus – from Meiringen and Grindelwald to Schwarzwaldalp

This is a walk that can be enjoyed by walkers of all abilities, exploring gently sloping meadows, woodland paths, waterfalls and a riverside walk on the return to Schwarzwaldalp. In addition to the optional stop for refreshments, there are canyons and waterfalls to visit at Hotel Rosenlaui, and an historic water-powered sawmill can be seen in action at Schwarzwaldalp. Although less visited from the Grindelwald side of Grosse Scheidegg, the Rychenbach valley is well worth exploring.

Buses run to Schwarzwaldalp from Grindelwald and Meiringen. From the bus stop at **Schwarzwaldalp** walk down the road for 600 metres and take a track to the left immediately before a bridge where the road crosses the Rychenbach river. The track rises to pass just below a collection of alp buildings and chalets then descends into pine woods, becoming a delightful path with occasional views up to the mountain wall on the other side of the valley.

Emerging into a gently sloping pasture dotted with occasional deciduous trees, a bench mid-way across provides an opportunity to enjoy an uninterrupted view of the mountain wall across the valley.

The **views** open up, and a steep rocky hanging valley can clearly be seen, with the Rosenlaui glacier high up. To the right are the Klein Wellhorn and Wellhorn, while to the left of the hanging valley,

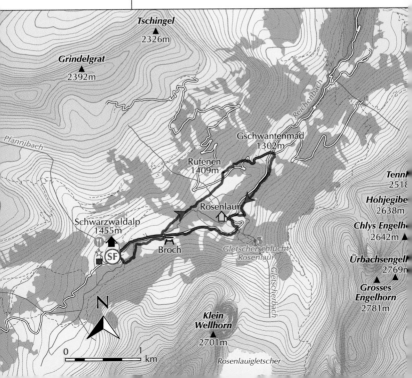

vast grey contorted walls and spires rise to the Chlys
and Grosses Engelhorn, Hohjegiburg and Tennhorn
which dominate the scene.

*Views across
the valley to the
mountains above
Rosenlaui*

After 30min come to a road and cross straight over
continuing onto a grassy path, then at **Rufenen** (1409m)
take the path right signed to Gschwantenmad.

Descend on the track, then at a point where the track
crosses a stream keep left through a gate with a yellow
footpath symbol. (A minor road goes through a tunnel on
the other side of the stream). Descend to cross straight
over the road, and cross again then continue down on the
road to the farming hamlet of **Gschwantenmad** (1302m,
45min).

Cross the main valley road and the river and take
the riverside path to the right heading back uphill. This
is a lovely part of the walk, with the river next to the
path across meadows and through woods. After 4.3km,
1hr 15min, cross a stream, pass through a farm (cheese
and jam on sale) and cross the Rychenbach river to the
impressive looking **Rosenlaui Hotel**, situated by the
road next to a bridge. Refreshments. Here you can take
an optional excursion to view the Gletscherschlucht
Rosenlaui (glacier waterfall canyons). ▶

The gorge at
Gletscherschlucht
Rosenlaui can be
viewed from a well-
constructed path,
is free of charge
and open from
May to October.

From the hotel cross the river once more on the road, then take the path up to the right through pine woods and across meadows with the road always close or just below.

At **Broch**, where the road crosses the river, keep with the river on your right and pass a picnic area, then follow the beautiful path beside the river up to a bridge, cross over and arrive at **Schwarzwaldalp** (1455m, 2hr). Hotel, restaurant, bus stop.

SCHWARZWALDALP

The working sawmill at Schwarzwaldalp is fascinating to watch

A sawmill at Schwarzwaldalp has stood on the same site since 1800, and the current mill is dated 1896. A planing machine was installed in 1947 making it possible to produce finished goods on the site, and this is the only water-powered planer in Switzerland. The water wheel is 3.4m in diameter and makes around 18–20 revolutions per minute. Logs are clamped to a cradle which is moved towards the saw which rises up and down, powered through a series of wheels, gearing and pulleys. A foundation established in 1997 has ensured the sawmill continues to be operational, producing chopping boards and ornamental products for sale on site and in nearby stores.

WALK 14

Meiringen – Grosse Scheidegg –
Grindelwald on the Via Alpina

Start	Meiringen 595m
Finish	Grindelwald 1040m
Distance	23.5km
Total ascent	1440m
Total descent	1000m
Grade	2
Time	8hr
Max altitude	1962m at Grosse Scheidegg
Refreshments	Meiringen, Zwirgi, Rosenlaui, Schwarzwaldalp, Grosse Scheidegg, Hotel Wetterhorn, Grindelwald
Access	Train to Interlaken and then Meiringen, or bus over Grosse Scheidegg, changing at Schwarzwaldalp. Both take about 1hr 15min

This approach to Grindelwald from the east is a part of the classic Alpine Pass Route – the Via Alpina, Swiss Route 1 – that traverses Switzerland from Sargans in the east through to Montreux on Lac Léman. This is a long way and certainly a full day, but the route is never far from a relieving bus if required and this provides freedom to tailor the route as you wish.

Meiringen is home to the Reichenbach falls, where Sherlock Holmes took the criminal mastermind Moriarty to their mutual doom (or did he?). In a land of vast falls of water, these are interesting rather than impressive but suffice to serve their literary purpose.

The Meiringen valley is quite different from the Grindelwald side, calmer, undeveloped apart from a few mountain restaurants. Grindelwald buses go to Grosse Scheidegg and Schwarzwaldalp providing transport if desired.

Take the train from Interlaken to **Meiringen**. Turn right from Meiringen's train station, and right again on the main street. Pass sculptures of Holmes and the great guide Melchior Anderegg, apparently short roping his

English client, the alpinist Leslie Stephens. Follow the road as it turns and cross a bridge. Keep left at the round-about, and in 400m turn right just after the funicular to the Reichenbach Falls and Hotel Tourismus in the 'sub-urb' of **Willigen** (20min).

Take a narrow road past houses and follow the path as it starts to climb steeply, past more houses and a farm building. Cross the road, the first of several cross-ings on this lower section. Climb a cobbled track, again this will become familiar, pass the hamlet of **Schwendi** (791m, hotel with possible refreshments), and continue

1891   1991

• AT THIS FEARFUL PLACE,
SHERLOCK HOLMES
VANQUISHED PROFESSOR
MORIARTY, ON 4 MAY 1891.

• AN DIESEM
FURCHTERREGENDEN ORT
BESIEGTE SHERLOCK
HOLMES AM 4. MAI 1891
PROFESSOR MORIARTY.

• A CET ENDROIT
TERRIFIANT, SHERLOCK
HOLMES A VAINCU LE
PROFESSEUR MORIARTY
LE 4 MAI, 1891.

Erected by ★ errichtet von ★ erigé par
The Bimetallic Question of Montréal and
The Reichenbach Irregulars of Switzerland.

A small plaque marks the spot where Sherlock Holmes defeated the evil Professor Moriarty at the Reichenbach Falls

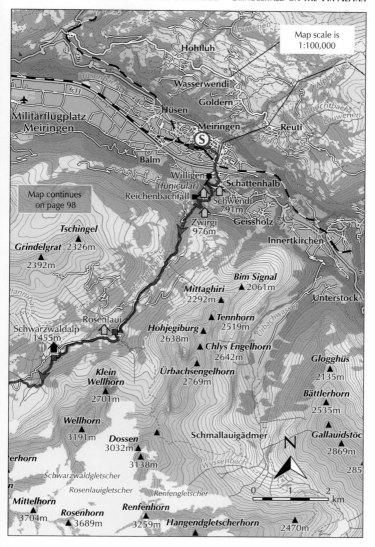

Map scale is
1:100,000

Louwenen

Hohfluh

Wasserwendi

Goldern

Hüsen

Meiringen

Reuti

Militärflugplatz
Meiringen

Balm

Willigen
(funicular)
Reichenbachfall

Schattenhalb

Schwendi
791m

Geissholz

Map continues
on page 98

Zwirgi
976m

Innertkirchen

Tschingel

Grindelgrat 2326m

2392m

Bim Signal
▲ 2061m

Mittaghiri
2292m

Unterstock

Tennhorn
▲ 2519m

Rosenlaui

Hohjegiburg
2638m

Chlys Engelhorn
2642m

Schwarzwaldalp
1455m

Ürbachsengelhorn
2769m

Glogghüs
▲
2135m

Klein
Wellhorn
2701m

Bättlerhorn
▲
2535m

Wellhorn
3191m

Dossen
3032m

Schmallauigädmer

Gallauidstöc
▲
2869m

3138m

Wyssenbach

N

285

erhorn

Schwarzwaldgletscher

Rosenlauigletscher

Renfengletscher

0   1   2   km

Mittelhorn
3704m

Rosenhorn
▲ 3689m

Renfenhorn
3259m

Hangendgletscherhorn

▲
2470m

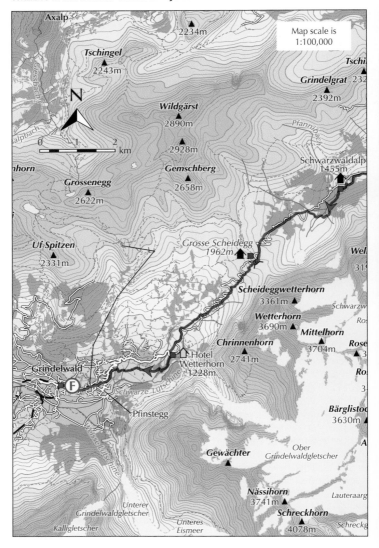

Map scale is
1:100,000

the ascent through woods and pastures, coming to the **Reichenbach Falls** (845m, 1hr).

Climb the steep path to pass the falls, seeing the plaque of the exact spot where the alleged deed happened. Continue to climb and come to the road and the hotel at **Zwirgi** (976m, 1hr 30min).

Cross the road at the hairpin and take the trail that climbs above the road on the cobbled (mule) track. Initially climb above the road but the road and path intersect several times and soon there is a 1km section of road (passing another restaurant). Continue the dance with the road, coming to a level area. Keep left at a bridge to the farming hamlet of Gschwantenmad where other paths are signed right. This enters a delightful section alongside the Reichenbach stream, emerging by the **Rosenlaui Hotel** (1328m, 3hr).

The ramparts of the Wellhorn tower above Schwarzwaldalp

Cross the bridge and climb past a café. The path keeps above the road, before branching away for another section alongside the river, coming to a bridge to reach **Schwarzwaldalp**, with buses and a restaurant (1455m, 3hr 45min).

Continue above Schwarzwaldalp into pastures. Head into woods and cross a narrow bridge. Follow the path through woods before coming to a road crossing. From here the route climbs steadily, not steeply, towards **Grosse Scheidegg**, crossing the road numerous times before arriving at the famous pass and convenient restaurant (1962m, 5hr 30min).

To continue to Grindelwald, follow the path down. This also crosses the road numerous times before arriving at the **Hotel Wetterhorn** (1228m, 7hr). For Grindelwald, take the path at the far end of the parking area and follow into Grindelwald, on tracks through woods, with occasional short ascents, arriving tired but happy in **Grindelwald** (1040m, 8hr).

ROUTES INTO THE MOUNTAIN WALL

Looking down into the deep Gletscherschlucht on the route to the Marmorbruch berggasthaus (Walk 16)

WALK 15
The Gleckstein Hut

Start	Gleckstein bus stop on the Grosse Scheidegg road (1557m)
Finish	Hotel Wetterhorn (1228m)
Distance	10.5km
Total ascent	900m
Total descent	1230m
Grade	4
Time	5hr
Max altitude	2316m, Gleckstein Hut
Refreshments	Gleckstein Hut, Hotel Wetterhorn
Access	Bus from Gridelwald to Gleckstein bus stop

Base for climbs on the Wetterhorn and Schreckhorn, the Gleckstein Hut is situated in a very dramatic position high above the Oberer Grindelwaldgletscher on the slopes of the Wetterhorn. The approach to it is steep and somewhat arduous and should not be tackled by inexperienced walkers. Whilst it's perfectly feasible to walk all the way from Grindelwald, most hut visitors take the bus as far as the bus stop on the way to Grosse Scheidegg. The described route returns to the Hotel Wetterhorn.

From the bus stop take the signed path towards the Wetterhorn. Pass a **1593m path junction** (later used on the descent) and keep straight ahead, cross a gully (often snow-choked throughout the walking season), and follow the path angling across the mountainside. This is protected by fixed cables as you climb above bare slabs with increasingly significant drops to the right. Turn an exposed corner to gain a view into the Upper Grindelwald glacier's gorge and pass above remains of a one-time cable car station, **Engi** (1hr).

This was one of the first **cable cars** in the valley but was uncommercial. The control room has been transplanted to the Grindelwald Museum and is well worth a visit.

The trail slopes downhill, then rises again to pass beneath a waterfall (an involuntary shower is inevitable). Shortly after, the way zigzags up a steep slope to find more fixed cables across steeply angled slabs. Come onto a grass-covered bluff at 2060m. The trail kinks left and climbs by ledges protected by a tubular metal handrail, and continues up grass slopes to reach the **Gleckstein Hut** (2hr 45min).

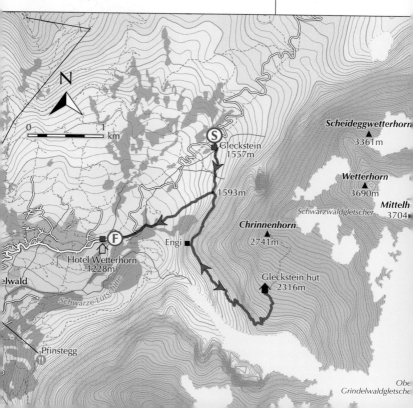

The walk to the Gleckstein Hut is exposed but not especially difficult (Photo: Joe Williams)

The **Gleckstein Hut** has a wonderful outlook. To the northeast the crags of the Wetterhorn rise in a confusion of rock and snow, while to the southeast the Schreckhorn appears above a turmoil of ice. Owned by the Burgdorf Section of the SAC it can accommodate 16 in four-bedded rooms, and 80 in dormitories. There is a resident guardian from the end of June to the end of September, when meals are available. For reservations Tel 033 853 11 40, www.gleckstein.ch.

From the hut there are marked routes southeast to Beesibärgli for an intimate view of the glaciers (2hrs); and north for the ascent of the 2737m Chrinnenhorn in 1hr 30min.

Continuing the way you started and returning to the bus stop is 20min shorter, but you will need to take the bus for a well-deserved beer.

Descend the same way, taking care on the exposed sections, which are protected by cables. Pass Engi, continuing to take care. At the 1593m path junction, turn left and descend through the Ischboden pastures and a final short section of road to the **Hotel Wetterhorn** (1228m, 5hr). ◀

WALK 16

Grindelwald – Pfingstegg – Hotel Wetterhorn circuit

Start/Finish	Grindelwald Bahnhof 1040m
Distance	14km
Total ascent	680m
Total descent	680m
Grade	2
Time	4hr 30min
Max altitude	1392m at Pfingstegg
Refreshments	Gletscherschlucht, Marmorbruch, Pfingstegg, Milchbach (closed in 2021), Hotel Wetterhorn

Pfingstegg sits on a ledge of pasture 350m above Grindelwald. Although it can be reached by cable car, this route explores the gorge of the Unterer Grindelwaldgletscher, a deep incision made by the Schwarze Lütschine, far below the path before climbing to Pfingstegg. From here the route traverses the slopes of the Mättenberg before dropping down to the Hotel Wetterhorn. The route can be shortened by taking the cable car down at Pfingstegg, in which case the walking route takes a little over 2hr for 6km of walking, with a climb of 520m.

From the *Bahnhof* cross the road and take the narrow path steeply downhill. This is marked with a green 1 for the Via Alpina 1 route. Continue down the hill with the Eiger looming above. Turn left after the Hotel des Glaciers. After bends cross the bridge and continue for 400m and after a right-hand bend, take a waymarked left turn signed to Trychelegg. At first a road, this climbs between houses before crossing a bridge and emerging into fields. Take either the road or the higher path and pass through the hamlet of **Trychelegg**.

Continue, at first across pasture, then entering a forest. The path climbs and contours for nearly 2km; it is usually good but with some roots to navigate. Turn left at the first path junction and then right where an ascending path joins. Drop down to the viewpoint high above the gorge.

> The **Gletscherschlucht gorge** is a tremendous feature, carved by the waters of the Weisse Lütschine and the glacier above. The views from above are spectacular, and it is possible (for a small fee) to enter the bottom of the gorge from the Gletscherschlucht hotel.

Cross the bridge and soon come to the **Marmorbruch berggasthaus** (1107m, 1hr 20min), well-sited for coffee or lunch.

The ascending path above the Marmorbruch is good and climbs the 300m in around 50min. The lower path climbs in zigzags, higher up, the woods thin. Pass a junction (**Wysseflüö**, 1380m). The right turn heads higher into the gorge and the Bäregg Hut (see Walk 17), keep left to traverse under cliffs to **Pfingstegg** (1392m, 2hr 20min).

The Marmorbruch looks out over Grindelwald

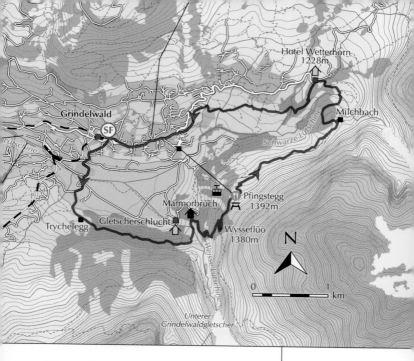

Pfingstegg has a restaurant overlooking the valley and fine views over Grindelwald and across to the Faulhorn. Play areas and animal petting are available. Descent is possible on the cable car to shorten the route.

Continue past the restaurant and descend on a track. After 400m take a path to the right that contours the mountainside and goes through a tunnel under a rock band. Continue traversing and descending and pass signs indicating that the hillside above is crumbling. At one point the path is diverted under an area where the path has been closed by rockfall. Climb back and join a more level track.

Pass signs to the **Milchbach** restaurant. If it is open, then climb the track for 100m to reach it. ▶ If closed, as

The views to the west flank of the Wetterhorn are spectacular and paths climb above the restaurant with views of the Oberer Grindelwaldgletscher.

it has been in recent years, then the restaurant is a sad place.

Descend back to the track and continue down with yellow Wanderweg signs. Cross an elegant bridge and turn left, following the track left and soon arriving in the substantial car park at the **Hotel Wetterhorn** (1228m, 3hr 30min). Refreshments.

From the hotel find the small sign at the far corner of the car park. Descend steadily on a track, taking a hard right waymarked turn after 500m onto a path. This continues to drop, crosses a stream, and emerges into pastures. Cross these, turn left then immediately right at a tarmacked track and continue along the signed small roads steadily descending to Grindelwald. Join the main street shortly before the First cable car station and continue through the village past hotels and shops to return to **Grindelwald Bahnhof** (1040m, 4hr 30min).

WALK 17
Pfingstegg – Bäregg Hut

Start/Finish	Pfingstegg 1392m
Distance	5.5km including return
Total ascent	460m to the hut, 40m on return walk
Total descent	460m
Grade	2–3
Time	3hrs, 1hr 30min each direction
Max altitude	1772m at the Bäregg Hut
Refreshments	Pfingstegg, Bäregg Hut
Access	Cable car to Pfingstegg

The short route leads into the heart of the mountains above Grindelwald and the gorge of the former Unterer Grindelwaldgletscher. The Bäregg hut, replacement for the older Steiregg hut destroyed by rockfall, sits high on a shelf overlooking the glacier. The position is most impressive, clearly visible from Grindelwald, surrounded by peaks and glaciers. The Finsteraarhorn and Fiescherhorn's glaciers tumble down whilst you also get some feel for the 'other side' of the Eiger.

The walk can be done in half a day, or to take in lunch at the hut. Another option is to stay overnight, especially in good weather when evening alpenglow and dawn on the peaks makes for a memorable experience.

For those not used to the scale, steepness, and drop-offs on alpine paths, this makes a good taster as you find your mountain legs.

From the **Pfingstegg** cable car station turn right past the play area and a small pasture. Descend gradually keeping close under the cliffs with water usually dripping a little. After 10min come to the junction with paths at **Wyssefluö** (1380m).

The route can be extended by walking up one of the many routes from **Grindelwald** (see Walk 16), either via the gorge to this path junction or more directly to Pfingstegg, adding around 1hr 30min to the ascent.

The route to the Bäregg Hut contours high above the gorge of the Unterer Grindelwaldgletscher on a good path

Steep cliffs on both sides draw the eye down to the gorge, whilst the views ahead open out into the vast cirque of peaks.

The path climbs and contours. Below, the deep gorge of the Gletscherschlucht steadily widens. ◄

The path is well made and much used. In a few places railings protect the unwary from the drops far below, but this is a good path for walkers of all standards. Young children seem to skip happily along, perhaps headed to their first night in the mountains, and what a night.

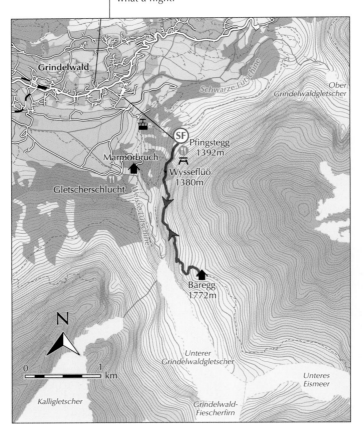

Lunch on the terrace of the welcoming Bäregg Hut

On a hot day the walk can seem longer than it actually is. Spot a Swiss flag after 1hr that indicates the position of the hut. For the last km, the route climbs steeply up grassy slopes before levelling off just before the **Bäregg Hut** (1772m, 1hr 30min). ▸

Take time to absorb the views and enjoy the facilities that the hut has to offer.

To descend, reverse the route. It will likely feel easier on the way down, but take care and enjoy the different views of the gorge and Grindelwald far below. Add an hour if you decide to walk down rather than taking the cable car, whilst a further option would be to turn left at Wysseflüö to the Marmorbruch restaurant and the crossing of the canyon, which would add 1hr 30min.

WALK 18

The Schreckhorn Hut

Start	Pfingstegg (1392m)
Finish	Schreckhorn Hut (2527m)
Distance	8.0km (one way), 16km round trip
Total ascent	1400m (outward), 1660m round trip
Total descent	260m (outward), 1660m round trip
Grade	4
Time	4–5hrs one way, 10hrs round trip
Max altitude	2527m at the Schreckhorn Hut
Refreshments	Pfingstegg, Bäregg Hut, Schreckhorn Hut
Access	Cable car to Pfingstegg, or walk from Grindelwald

The continuation of Route 17 is a much more demanding affair and should only be tackled by experienced mountain walkers. This is certainly the hardest walk in this book. Do not attempt it following heavy rainfall, or on especially hot days when stone fall danger is at its greatest.

Between Berghaus Bäregg and the Rots Gufer sections of the path may be liable to change, while mounting the slabs of the Rots Gufer ups the ante considerably, and calls for a good head for heights. Although safeguarded with fixed ladders, cables and metal pegs, the cliffs are steep and exposed. At the end of a challenging 5hr walk, the Schreckhorn Hut sits below the Schreckhorn's broken west face and overlooks a vast sweep of glacier with the Finsteraarhorn rising like a delicate fin to the south.

Follow Route 17 as far as **Berghaus Baregg** (accommodation, refreshments). Now descend slightly and cross a glacial basin (diverting up and down briefly to negotiate the eroded moraine) to reach a superb viewpoint on the ridge at 1800m. From here, the route turns east and undulates across grassy slopes (with another tiresome erosion diversion) to the base of the vertiginous **Rots Gufer**.

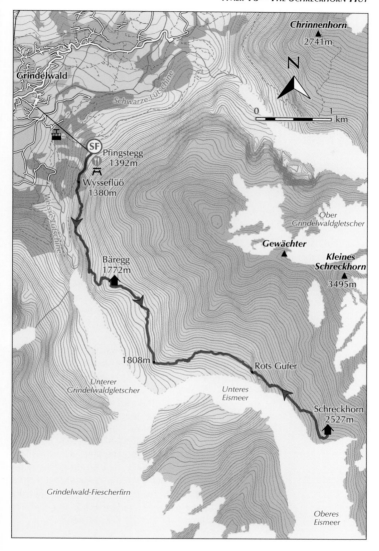

The Fiescherwand and Eiger (Photo: Caroline Holmes)

The **way up the cliffs** is well-marked and made safe with various aids, although caution must always be exercised. Roped parties are not uncommon here; the additional safeguard of a rope may be helpful as a slip would be very serious.

Above the Rots Gufer rock barrier the path continues, a little easier now, to cross streams and old snow patches (beware avalanches early in the season, or after snowfall). Then come to a cone of moraine and rocks spreading from the left. There are the ruins of a stone hut and beyond these the way seems to be blocked by converging glaciers. The path forks and you bear left to see the Schreckhorn Hut directly above. The final approach is along a slope of moraine. Built to replace the Strahlegg Hut, which was destroyed by avalanche, the **Schreckhorn Hut** is owned by the Basel Section of the SAC and has a resident guardian from late June to the end of September. There are 65 dormitory places and meals provided. For reservations Tel 033 855 10 25, www.sac-basel.ch.

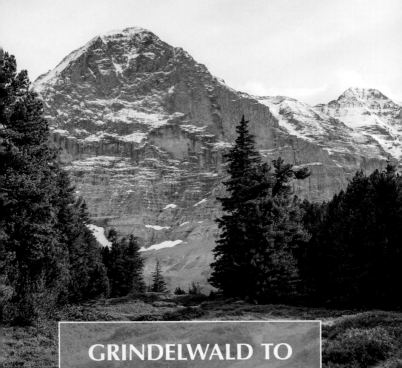

GRINDELWALD TO KLEINE SCHEIDEGG

Autumn colours and the Eiger on the Romantic Way between Männlichen and Alpiglen (Walk 22)

WALK 19
Grindelwald – Kleine Scheidegg –
Wengen – Lauterbrunnen

Start	Grindelwald Grund station 943m
Finish	Lauterbrunnen station 795m
Distance	19km
Total ascent	1120m
Total descent	1270m
Grade	2
Time	6–7hrs
Max altitude	2061m at Kleine Scheidegg
Refreshments	Brandegg, Alpiglen, Kleine Scheidegg, Wengernalp, Wengen, Lauterbrunnen
Access	Grund is the Kleine Scheidegg station, either walk down from Grindelwald Bahnhof (15min) or take train or bus. Return by train or cable car

This route cuts through the mountains between Grindelwald and Lauterbrunnen taking the Via Alpina Swiss Route 1 all the way. It's a majestic route, with views of most of the Oberland mountains, especially the Eiger as the route passes beneath on the ascent and the Jungfrau on the descent. It's clear and easy to follow but there is a fair amount of up and down and some may want to shorten the route. This is easy as the route is shared with the train system between Grindelwald and Lauterbrunnen, with changes at Kleine Scheidegg and Wengen as well as smaller stations, so you can use the trains as you wish to shorten the route.

From **Grindelwald Grund station** (a 5min train ride or 15min walk below the centre of the village), cross the river on the new road bridge and turn left past the car park. At the far end continue on Engelhausweg (not well signed at the time of research, and other paths start hereabouts too) which immediately starts to climb.

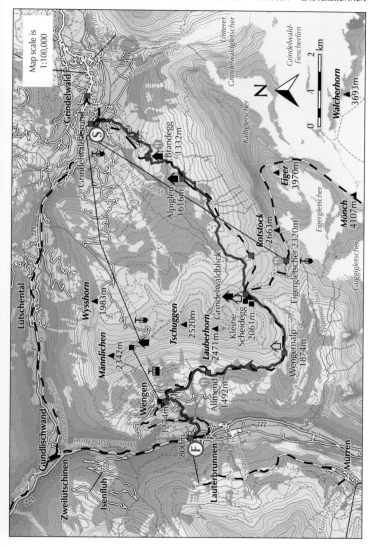

The road climbs past chalets. After 5min cross the railway tracks and come to a road, turn right and then in 20m left on Brandeggstrasse. Pass a kindergarten and take the footpath left. Now climb steadily on a well way-marked steeply climbing path. The signage at the bottom is mostly yellow Wanderweg signs rather than Route 1 signs but there are a few reassuring markers. ◄

By this point you have cracked most of the navigation difficulties on the route.

You are soon past chalets and then pass small farms and big barns, climbing close to the Sandbach steam. Cross the road several times as the path cuts off the loops of road. Shortly before Brandegg, the path follows the road round a big bend and goes under a bridge under the track before coming to the redeveloped hotel and *Berggasthaus* at **Brandegg** (1332m, 1hr 10min). ◄

Once the redevelopment is complete the route here may be further altered.

Continue on the road a short way above Brandegg before taking a track that climbs towards the Eiger. Pass farm buildings of Ober Brandegg and continue, now near the railway line. Pass through a short tunnel under the railway and climb steeply to the restaurant and *Berggasthaus* at **Alpiglen** (1616m, 2hr).

ALPIGLEN

Alpiglen was the waiting station for the intrepid mainly German and Austrian climbers who sought glory on the Eiger in the 1930s, sometimes playing a cat and mouse game with the Swiss authorities who for a time tried to ban climbers from the mountain. A memorial to these and many others lost on the famous and stern-looking north face is just above the hotel just off the route.

The story of these climbs has been told many times, perhaps best of all in Heinrich Harrer's book The White Spider, documenting his own first ascent with Heckmair, Vorg, and Kasparek and other even more traumatic experiences before and since.

Continue to climb above Alpiglen on a broad track that services the railway. Cross it 400m after the hotel. At the Mettla farm buildings briefly walk on tarmac before the track continues. Above the Arvengarten ski station, keep left and continue the final push to **Kleine Scheidegg** (2061m, 3hr 30min).

Kleine Scheidegg is where the tracks all meet, from Grindelwald, Wengen and down from Eigergletscher. It's usually a busy spot, although the new cable car from Grindelwald has taken much of the direct Jungfraujoch traffic.

Many paths leave Kleine Scheidegg, but the Wengen path is a major one and descends by the rail tracks and past a maintenance building. The Jungfrau is truly splendid seen from here. It is possible you will hear and see icefalls and avalanches from the lower slopes of the Jungfrau. ▶ Pass **Wengernalp** hotel and restaurant and station but keep to the track that steadily makes its way down to Wengen in slightly over 1hr 30min. Views across to Mürren, up the hill to Männlichen, across to the Lobhorn and glimpses of views down to Wengen fill the horizon. Pass the **Allmend restaurant**, keep left at the next junction and follow the tiny traffic-free road past hotels, to the station and so into the centre of **Wengen** (1274m, 5hr).

The attractive Allmend restaurant on the descent towards Wengen

You are now on a section of the path that is termed the Mendelssohnweg after the composer.

Downtown Wengen with its shops and hotels, trains and underpass

WENGEN

Wengen is well known as a ski resort, but without the apparent mechanical lifts common elsewhere. Several larger and smaller hotels as well as chalets, and great summer walking make this an attractive base.

To continue the descent to Lauterbrunnen, loop under the railway tracks. Descend steeply following the yellow signs round the twisting lanes of lower Wengen. The road becomes a track and continues down in innumerable zigzags. Soon Lauterbrunnen is seen below through the trees. At 1020m cross under a disused trackway and 100m lower cross the railway tracks on a new bridge. Lauterbrunnen, with its transport facilities and waterfalls is now clearly seen. Keep right at two turns and descend past a care home, come to a T-junction, turn right, pass a sports facility and school building. Turn left across a narrow footbridge over the Weisse Lütschine, then right again, pass under the railway station to emerge in **Lauterbrunnen** (800m, 6hr).

The main facilities in Lauterbrunnen Dorf and the spectacular waterfalls are to the left. Return to Grindelwald, if that is the plan, is by train or cable car from Wengen.

WALK 20

Grindelwald to Alpiglen the hard way

Start	Grindelwald 1040m
Finish	Alpiglen 1616m
Distance	9.25km
Total ascent	880m
Total descent	300m
Grade	3
Time	4hr
Max altitude	1760m
Refreshments	Gletscherschlucht hotel/Gasthaus, Alpiglen
Access	From the railway station at Grindelwald

There are several ways to Alpiglen, including the train and the Swiss Route 1 (see Walk 19). But this is different, with considerable ascent and some exposure as the route skirts the gorge of the Unterer Grindelwaldgletscher and then passes close under the bottom rocks of the Eiger's Mittellegi Ridge before dropping down to the welcome comforts of the restaurant at Alpiglen.

The route can be combined with Walk 21 which continues along the Eiger Trail to its high point at Eigergletscher. This makes for a full but worthwhile mountain day. Even if continuing, a stop at Alpiglen is still recommended to refresh for the higher trail.

This is a good morning route as the climb is entirely in shadow, but it may be cool outside the high summer season.

From **Grindelwald Bahnhof**, take Swiss Route 1 by the bus station. This descends steeply. Turn left just after the Les Glaciers hotel and continue to drop to the river. Turn left across the bridge (15min) and immediately left alongside the river. This skirts a works site and starts to climb coming to the **Gletscherschlucht hotel** (1014m, 35min).

Climb directly above the hotel. After 10min keep right where the path from the Marmorbruch hotel joins and in a further 10min keep left where another path

The trees thin and looking ahead there seems to be no way through, just a wall of rock with tree-covered ledges, yet the path finds a way.

joins. Signs warn sternly that the path is unsuitable for dogs. Pass a rocky viewpoint after 1hr 15min with views back to Grindelwald. ◀

Come to a section with chain and then a ladder and climb to a totally unexpected shelter in a clearing (**Lägerli**, 1508m) after 1hr 45min. From here the path starts its long traverse with continual ups and downs, initially in woods, then with a cabled section and under cliffs with substantial caves, the path makes its way westwards. Pass a substantial open area under cliffs (**Schüssellaui**, which the sign claims is 1545m, but is probably nearer 1600m.

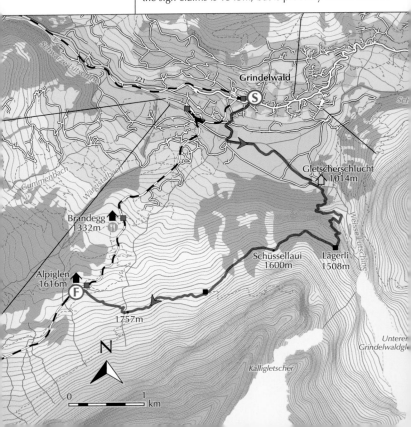

The route eases now, sometimes in trees sometimes on open hillside at the foot of the Eiger. Cross four streams, now above the trees on grassy hillsides. Pass a shelter (3hr 15min). In a further 20min come to the junction with the Eiger Trail signpost 1757m (3hr 40min) and turn right to descend the 140m in 15–20min to arrive at **Alpiglen** (1616m, 4hrs).

Looking back to the Wetterhorn and Grosse Scheidegg from Alpiglen

WALK 21

*The Eiger Trail – Alpiglen to Eigergletscher
and Kleine Scheidegg*

Start	Alpiglen 1616m
Finish	Eigergletscher 2320m
Distance	6km to/from Eigergletscher, 8.5km to/from Kleine Scheidegg
Total ascent	780m
Total descent	80m (260m extra to Kleine Scheidegg)
Grade	2–3
Time	2hr 50min to Eigergletscher in ascent, 2hr in descent. Extra time if starting/finishing at Kleine Scheidegg 50min going up and 40min down
Max altitude	2320m at Eigergletscher
Refreshments	Alpiglen, Eigergletscher, Kleine Scheidegg
Access	Train to Alpiglen and walk up or cable car to Eigergletscher

The Eiger Trail is one of the great walks of the area. In years past it was a high mountain route, but the new lift system to Eigergletscher has greatly improved access and the path has likewise been improved. Maybe some of the challenge has been lost, but the access is welcome and the situation, right under the famous north face, hasn't changed. The route can be done from either direction, a descent from the top station to Alpiglen is also described below.

In good weather there are few concerns. If the weather is bad, it might be better to wait for another day, not least as you will not see the magnificent, if foreshortened, cliffs of the Eiger.

Up or down? Up arguably gives a greater feel for the north face and the slopes are not steep. But it is quite possible you will have visited the Jungfraujoch 'Top of Europe' complex between the Jungfrau and Mönch (expensive but a great experience, especially if it is clear and you are able to make the walk across the glacier to the Mönchsjochhütte). After this, the walk down under the Eiger is a great way to finish the day.

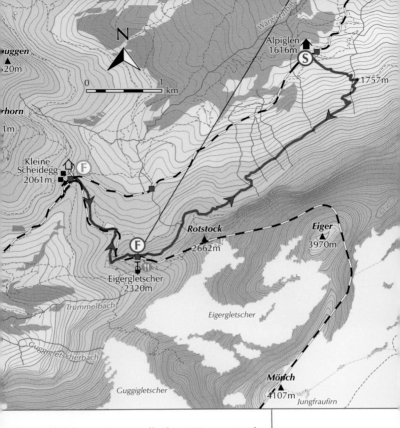

From **Alpiglen** station, walk the 100m up to the *Berggasthaus* and then through, finding a sign that indicates Eigergletscher in 2hr 50min. Take the good path that slopes uphill, first through alpine pasture and then into rockier terrain. After 20min, come to a **path junction** (1757m).

Turn right uphill. (The path left takes the high-level route back to Grindelwald, see Walk 20.) The path trends upwards, ever closer to the bottom rocks of the famous north face. It crosses rocks, but never with difficulties, and at a modest angle.

The (much foreshortened) view of the Eiger from high on the Eiger Trail

The view of the **Eiger** is highly foreshortened being so close under it. But this 'loss' is offset by the dramatic feeling of being (almost) on the brooding, renowned cliffs above. You can readily make out the traverse that Andreas Hinterstoisser made but couldn't recross, and the Eigerwand Station just above where Toni Kurz died so terribly of exhaustion on the same attempt in 1936. Willy Angerer and Edi Rainer also died in the attempt.

Despite the deadly happenings of the 1930s and beyond, the Eiger Trail remains a great walk, slanting uphill. After 1hr 45min, come to a bench(!) at the top of a scree.

Continue, initially uphill and then round a spur close under the cable car lines and then briefly downhill before making a final climb to the **Eigergletscher station**

(2320m, 2hr 50min). A lower route traverses below the station to join the Kleine Scheidegg path just below the top station.

Descent to Kleine Scheidegg

To descend to Kleine Scheidegg takes around 40min. The path down passes a relocated climbers hut, originally from the sharp east ridge of the Eiger – the Mittellegi ridge – with bedding, a dummy of a climber inside (and rope and pack outside). Views from here to the Jungfrau and Mönch are outstanding. Descend on the well-constructed tourist track, passing through a tunnel and the creatively developed ski-reservoir with Eiger memorial, before resuming on a track that leads directly to **Kleine Scheidegg** (2061m, 3hr 30min). Allow 40min in descent and 50min in ascent.

Eigergletscher to Alpiglen

Leave the terminal building (which could grace many airports), turn right and pass under the cable car lines and close under the cliffs. Descend on a path carved from the shale for 50m, before climbing again to a shoulder, passing

The Eiger Trail makes a high traverse right below the foot of the north face of the Eiger

close by the cable car lines, and a turn upwards to a via ferrata on the Eiger's lower cliffs. And pass a bench.

Continue down across a broad scree. The path then descends more gradually, traversing the slopes, crossing streams, and becoming grassier. A steeper descent leads to the **1757m path junction** (1hr 40min). Turn left and descend more steeply again to reach **Alpiglen** (1616m, 2hr).

WALK 22

Männlichen to Alpiglen, the Romantic Way – the Höhenweg 1900

Start	Männlichen 2222m
Finish	Alpiglen 1616m
Distance	7.5km
Total ascent	40m
Total descent	645m
Grade	2
Time	2hr
Max altitude	2222m Männlichen
Refreshments	Männlichen, Alpiglen
Access	Cable car from Wengen or gondola lift from Grindelwald Terminal, train from Alpiglen
Note	There is a standard combined ticket from Grindelwald that covers the gondola and train for this linear route

Also known as the Romanticweg (Romantic Way), this is a beautiful and interesting descent route which leads to Alpiglen. The walk can easily be completed within 2 hours, but why rush? For much of the walk a good mountain path descends easily across the eastern flank of Tschuggen, the hillsides covered with juniper, alpenrose and bilberries, with occasional lightly wooded areas – the alpenrose providing wonderful colour in early summer, while in late September the bilberry leaves turn the entire hillside fiery red. Views are tremendous ahead to the Eiger, across to the Wetterhorn and down into the Grindelwald valley. Although the final descent to Alpiglen is mainly on gravel tracks, the rest of the route more than compensates for this.

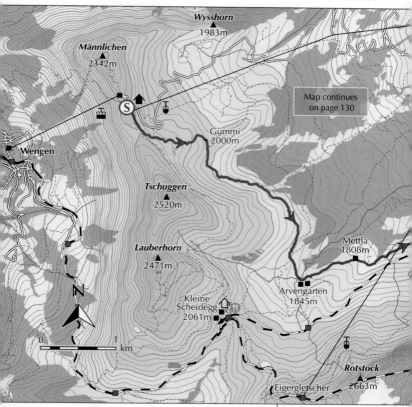

Exit the gondola top station at **Männlichen** and take the track that passes under the cables. Descend to a small col then turn left onto the Höhenweg 1900 signed to Alpiglen.

At first the walk is on a track, but changes to a path to descend and pass close to the higher Tschuggen ski lift. The path continues down in a steady gentle descent, meets a track, then shortly after at a point marked **Gummi** (2000m) leave the track and branch right onto

129

a wonderful path that descends across the hillside passing briefly through an area of boulders. The hillsides are covered in alpenrose, juniper and bilberry, with the Eiger and Mönch looming massively ahead. The path briefly divides, but both options join again, although the right hand (higher) fork is probably best.

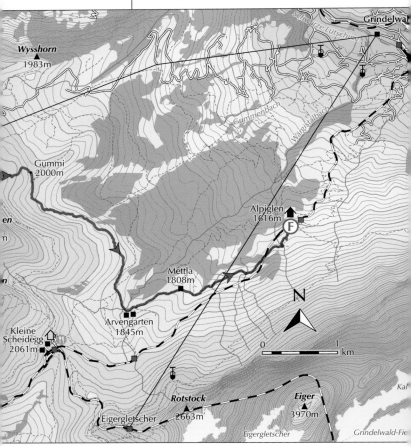

A walker approaches Bustiglen and Arvengarten

The delightful path passes through a lightly wooded area with Eiger views ahead, then finally meets a track. Turn right slightly uphill, then down to a group of buildings and then left to pass between two ski lift stations at **Arvengarten** (1845m), then rise to meet the main track leading down to Alpiglen.

After 5.4km the gravel track becomes a road that bends left at **Mettla** (1808m), at which point take the path to the right signed to Alpiglen which becomes a track again and continue descending. Cross the railway line, then walk down, passing a small sign to an Eiger memorial stone just before arriving in **Alpiglen** (1616m, 2hr). ▶

The Eiger memorial stone commemorates '50 years between 1938 and 1988 in memory of the casualties under the Eiger north face'.

The **Alpiglen Berghaus and restaurant** provides a warm welcome, with meals and snacks served throughout the day, and overnight accommodation provided in rooms and dormitories. Situated just beneath the north face of the Eiger, the location is very special. The train station at Alpiglen is about 100 metres to the west, below the *Berghaus*.

WALK 23

Männlichen to Kleine Scheidegg
Panoramaweg – the Höhenweg 2100

Start	Männlichen gondola station 2222m
Finish	Kleine Scheidegg 2061m
Distance	4.5km
Total ascent	20m
Total descent	180m
Grade	1
Time	1hr
Max altitude	2222m Männlichen
Refreshments	Männlichen, Grindelwaldblick, Kleine Scheidegg
Access	Cable car from Wengen, or gondola lift from Grindelwald Terminal. Train at Kleine Scheidegg

This walk is a classic, sometimes called the Panoramaweg or Höhenweg 2100, it is probably the easiest walk in this book. Although only just over 4km long, the superb views are constant, as the route threads its way around the hillsides full of flowers, heather and bilberries. As you draw nearer to Kleine Scheidegg, views of the massive north face of the Eiger, as well as the Mönch and Jungfrau are almost overwhelming. The route follows a broad gravel track with no difficulty, and a fine viewpoint with seating is reached just a short distance from Kleine Scheidegg.

To visit the Männlichen summit, turn north from the station and climb the surreptitiously steepening path to the viewpoint taking an extra 30min.

◀ Leave either the gondola (from Grindelwald) or cable car station (from Wengen) and walk south, passing underneath the Grindelwald gondola to find a broad track. Pass through a gate below the gondola station then fork right after 350 metres (the Romanticweg path to the left leads to Alpiglen). Now keep left, ignoring the steep path ahead. The path to follow goes gently downhill hugging the hillside, enjoying fine views.

At 2km the track rounds a promontory with the **Honegg** lift station ahead, pass beneath cables and reach

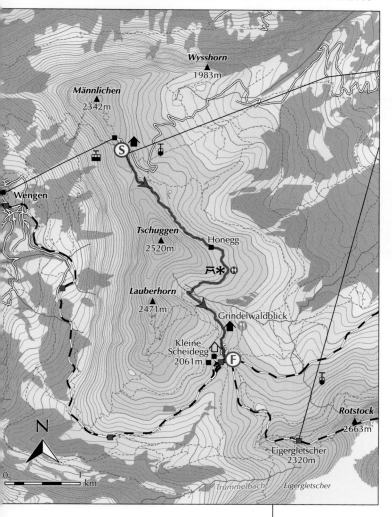

Superb views at the start of the walk from Männlichen

a viewpoint with benches (toilets available). Descend gently again and soon the buildings at Kleine Scheidegg come into view. Follow the path as it contours round one last bowl in the hillside, cross the Wärgischtalbach stream then climb to pass the **Grindelwaldblick Hotel and restaurant** which is set on a rocky knoll with a terrace and viewing platform. Finally walk down to reach **Kleine Scheidegg** at 2061m, 4.5km, 1hr.

WENGEN TO
KLEINE SCHEIDEGG

The view from the memorial is a little obscured by trees, probably Mendelssohn had a better view (Walk 28)

WALK 24
Kleine Scheidegg and Wengernalp

Start/Finish	Kleine Scheidegg 2061m
Alt start/finish	Wengernalp station 1874m
Distance	10km (alternative 7.5km)
Total ascent	460m (alternative 360m)
Total descent	460m (alternative 360m)
Grade	2
Time	3hr 30min (alternative 2hr 45min)
Max altitude	2062m
Refreshments	Kleine Scheidegg, Wengernalp, alp cheese etc at Eggplätz
Access	Train – starting from Grindelwald, Wengen or Lauterbrunnen
Note	An alternative shorter walk could start and finish at Wengernalp station, which can be shortened further by taking a short section of track between the farm at Eggplätz and Weiss Fluh

This walk is a fine outing exploring the moraine, pastures and woodlands below Wengernalp and Kleine Scheidegg. The huge and impressive rock faces of the Jungfrau loom above, while views to the southwest are to Mürren, the Schilthorn and Sefinafurgga pass on the far side of the Lauterbrunnen valley. The walk is described from Kleine Scheidegg, with an easy section at the start and end across broad pastures between Kleine Scheidegg and Haaregg, however the slightly shorter circular walk from Wengernalp may be preferred.

Leaving the station platform, walk towards the sports/ souvenirs shop and at the signed path cross the tracks, descending in a zigzag then more gently straight across a broad pasture. After 15min cross over a stream, then rise out of the stream bed and note a path right signed

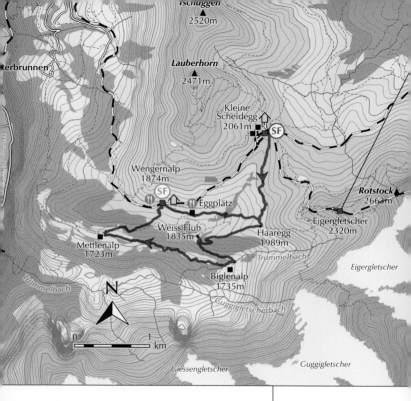

Wengernalp restaurant. This will be the path you return on. Ignoring this path to Wengernalp continue rising to the crest of an old moraine at **Haaregg** (1989m, 30min).

There are **fine views** all around from this vantage point, and several piles of stones mark the line of the crest of the moraine and path ahead.

Walk down the crest of the moraine, the path then descends more steeply, becoming rocky and stony, then swing left at a sign to drop more easily through light pine woods to reach **Weiss Fluh** (Wyssi Fluh on the SwissTopo map, 1835m, 1hr).

Cheeses and snacks available from a fridge near the farm at Eggplätz

There is a well-placed **bench** from which you can take in the views directly across the Lauterbrunnen valley to Mürren, with the Schilthorn and Sefinafurgga pass beyond.

Take the left hairpin path down through woods, cross a relatively level boulder-strewn pasture, then come to a sign to Stalden and Wengen. 1hr 15min.

Do not cross the obvious bridge, but keeping to the right of the streambed, descend gently through woodland (muddy in places) and occasional grassy hillsides. The path then begins to climb steadily, to reach a path junction and track at **Mettlenalp** (1723m, 2hr). Turn right up the track for a few metres then turn right again onto a rising path. At 1765m meet a track and turn right, then fork left on the path rising across pastures, then more steeply to reach **Wengernalp** (1874m, 2hr 30min).

For the train station, pass under the track and walk down to the station.

To continue the walk (or for the alternative start from Wengernalp station) take the gravel track that descends past a few farm buildings by the tunnel under the railway tracks. This descends gently to a hairpin bend and farm chalet at **Eggplätz** (cheese and other snacks from fridge). ▶

Pass to the right of the farm chalet on a path that rises steadily. Cross a stream then keeping the stream just to your left, continue uphill then under ski lift cables to meet the path from Kleine Scheidegg, (1975m, 3hr).

To return to Kleine Scheidegg turn left, retracing your earlier route. If walking the circular walk from Wengernalp, turn right to Haaregg, and continue with the route description after the first paragraph.

To take the shortcut to **Weiss Fluh** continue on the track past the Wengernalp Wixi ski lift.

WALK 25

Eigergletscher to Wengen by the moraine

Start	Eigergletscher 2320m
Finish	Wengen 1274m
Distance	11.5km
Total ascent	100m
Total descent	1150m
Grade	2–3
Time	3hr 30min
Max altitude	2320m at the start at Eigergletscher
Refreshments	Eigergletscher, then none on the route before Wengen
Access	Train or cable car to Eigergletscher or walk up from Kleine Scheidegg in 50min

From the Eigergletscher station, a long moraine extends west below the soaring rocks and tumbling glaciers of the Mönch and Jungfrau. You are likely to hear the groaning and cracking of the icefalls far above and to see the occasional avalanche coming down (a safe distance away). The upper section is on a narrow path right on the crest of the moraine; lower down the route makes a descent through mountain terrain, into forest and pasture before a delightful descent into Wengen.

The top 150m of the moraine is the only grade 3 challenge on the route. The moraine is generally over 1 metre wide with a good path down, although the slopes on either side may concern some. In this case the route can be accessed from the Kleine Scheidegg–Eigergletscher route and the top section missed out.

As with many of the routes, the path network gives lots of options to tailor your start and finish points. A start from Kleine Scheidegg is possible (Walk 30), and a finish down the Trümmelbach falls (Walk 28) is an option too.

Start on the platform of the railway station, where a sign indicates the walking options from **Eigergletscher**. Follow signs to Biglenalp. Cross the stony ground and climb directly to the moraine. Paths descend in the ablation valley to the right if you prefer, but the moraine is a solid route. Descend calmly.

The steep upper section of the moraine below Eigergletscher is not difficult

Avoiding the top of the moraine

Drop down the path to Kleine Scheidegg and at the prominently placed old Mittellegi ridge hut, turn left and

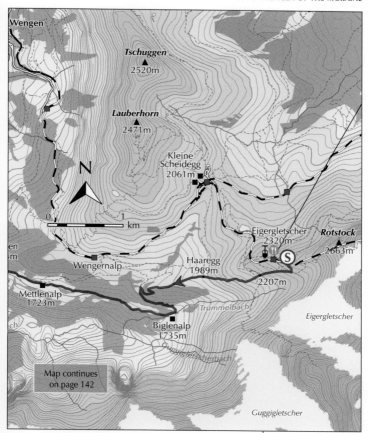

traverse the slopes to reach the route at the **path junction at 2207m**. If you start from Kleine Scheidegg this takes 45min to join the main route.

Main route

Continue down on less steep moraine to reach **Haaregg** (1989m, 30min). From here you can see Wengernalp

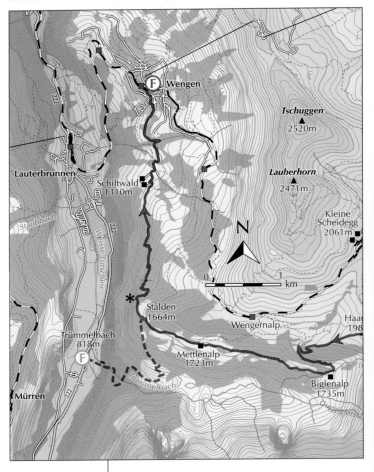

From here you can link with Walk 24.

with its hotel and station across the valley while to your left the Jungfrau dominates everything. ◄

Pass along an open ridge with views in all directions, then into an area of smaller trees and shrubs. This is an area called Weiss Fluh one of several in the region. The path twists and turns and at 1835m turn left at a junction. (Right would allow a quick return to Wengernalp). The path descends to **Biglenalp** (1735m, 1hr 15min) an area of open pasture with small buildings sited below the Jungfrau's ramparts.

Continue without crossing the bridge. The path undulates through forest and sometimes muddy pastures passing the farm buildings at **Mettlenalp** (1723m) where it joins a track for 15min before coming to **Stalden** (1664m, 2hr 10min). Here, take a small path down to a clearing and a further signpost. Left is to the Trümmelbach descent, whilst the Wengen path is straight ahead.

▶ A **viewpoint** at Staldenflue (1600m) provides tremendous views to the Jungfrau above and across the Lauterbrunnen valley. Continue on the path, there are no options, just peaceful woods and glimpses of great views, and an occasional peek ahead to Wengen. Come to the delightful farm buildings at **Schiltwald** (1310m) where the views of Wengen ahead are enticing.

You are now on one of the best routes around Wengen, dropping through the woods on a well-made path.

Join the tiny road to the right passing through meadows, there may be the occasional farm vehicle, but Wengen is largely traffic-free. ▶ Pass under the Allmend chairlift (weekends only in summer). Stay on the lane, it's the waymarked route, avoiding all temptations up and down, and soon cross under the railway and arrive in the centre of **Wengen** (1274m, 3hr 30min).

If anything, the lower buildings are even more photogenic.

WENGEN

The well-known winter ski resort of Wengen sits on a high shelf above the valley and has many hotels, restaurants, shops and other facilities. It makes a fine base for summer walking with transport links and routes giving access for many days' walking. The village is almost entirely traffic-free, and trains and lifts provide many options to Männlichen, Kleine Scheidegg and Eigergletscher as well as in the Lauterbrunnen valley below.

Trümmelbach descent

At Stalden take the path left, indicating 1hr 50min to the valley which is 800m below. Signs warn cyclists that this is beyond their capabilities. The descent is steep with ladders and cables and starts almost immediately, and as you near the bottom you will hear and pass the upper Trümmelbach falls before descending the bottom 150m where the path is carved from the cliff and protected by cables the whole way, arriving at the road. The hotel, its restaurant, and the bus stop are 200m to the right. To visit the falls costs 12CHF and is well worthwhile but after this big descent this may not be the first thing on your mind. (For more information see Walk 30).

WALK 26
Wengen – Leiterhorn circuit

Start/Finish	Wengen station 1276m
Distance	5.25km
Total ascent	240m
Total descent	240m
Grade	2
Time	1hr 45min
Max altitude	1520m
Refreshments	Wengen, none on route
Access	Train from Lauterbrunnen or Kleine Scheidegg or cable car from Männlichen

The Leiterhorn (Leiterharen on some maps) is a fantastic viewpoint high above Wengen, with picnic and barbeque facilities – a great destination. The walk described explores some of the smaller satellite settlements above Wengen, including An der Ledi that enjoys superb views along the length of the Lauterbrunnen valley and towards the snowy peaks above. The way up is steep from there onwards, mainly through beautiful pine woods to emerge at Leiterhorn. The route back to Wengen follows a broad gravel track for much of the way, allowing you to fix your eyes on the superb views for much of the time, before finally descending on pretty woodland paths which drop directly down into the main street of Wengen.

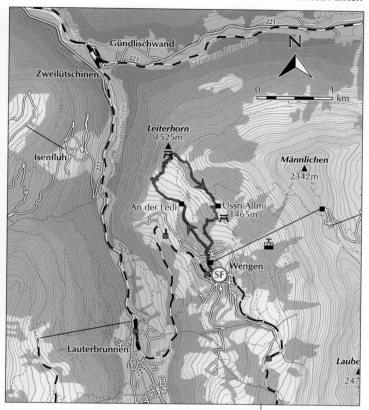

From the station walk up the main street, right past the Palace Hotel then left signed Leiterhorn. Climb on this road then after 0.7km, at 1423m reach a road junction by a large forestry building and turn left.

This level track takes you through the hamlet of **An der Ledi**, where every house has a view! After passing the last house, the path begins climbing towards woods, but then take a smaller path right just at the edge of the woods and continue to climb in zigzags. ▶

There are awesome views down into the Lauterbrunnen valley with the Mittaghorn, Grosshorn and Breithorn above and the ever-present Jungfrau on the left.

145

The Jungfrau dominates views into the Lauterbrunnen valley from near the Leiterhorn

To climb to the highest point, continue ahead through trees to the summit of Leiterhorn.

Continue climbing mainly through light pine woods to reach a well-placed bench, to enjoy the opportunity for a rest and admire the views. The beautiful woodland path continues to climb to reach a picnic area with barbecue at **Leiterhorn** (1500m, 1hr). ◀

Continue past the picnic area where there are two alternative return paths. Take the track ahead which rises to 1520m where it joins another track. Turn right and start descending.

When the track swings sharp right at **Ussri Allmi**, take the path left just after the bend and descend to a picnic area, cross the track and continue on the path, then veer right then immediately left to pass below a large modern chalet, then through a tiny gate (wanderweg sign) past another chalet. The path is now metalled as it passes between more chalets, descending steadily. At a path T junction go right down steeply to join the main road through **Wengen** (5.25km, 1hr 45min).

WALK 27

Wengen to Männlichen – the Gemsweg

Start	Wengen 1274m
Finish	Männlichen 2222m
Distance	5km
Total ascent	950m
Total descent	0m
Grade	3
Time	3hr
Max altitude	2222m at Männlichen
Refreshments	Wengen, then none until Männlichen
Access	Train from Lauterbrunnen or Kleine Scheidegg, cable car from Männlichen

It's called the Gemsweg (way of the Chamois) for very good reasons. This is a steep climb above Wengen to the Männlichen cable car station, and after halfway it becomes even steeper on the open hillside, with one explanatory board suggesting the slope is 80°. This seems too much, but it is certainly very steep. The path, however, is continuously good and is full of interest – the bottom sections climb on good paths through woodland and pine forest, whilst higher up the forest of avalanche protection is both interesting and, for those who might get exposed, reassuring.

From the *Bahnhof*, pass along the main street of Wengen. Keep left at the Hotel Schönegg and take the next right. The signs say Männlichen is over a 3hr walk. Walk up the road for 100m, then continue straight ahead, with signs for Ussri Allmi. The path turns left. Climb steadily past chalets including a substantial new construction. Come to a path junction at 1415m and climb through pasture. At a track junction turn right, take a hairpin, and come to the **Ussri Allmi** junction (1465m, 30min).

Turn right into woods. The path steadily becomes a graded (likely a mule) track gaining height at an acceptable gradient, passing the clearing of Hittenboden. At around 1650–1700m, the trees thin out and the path steepens. At 1700m the path takes a definite right turn with a prominent marker on a large rock out onto more open hillside. ◄ Climb to the **Parwengi** junction (1864m, 1hr 50min). Meet another path that climbed the woods to this point from near the Allmend restaurant.

Gaps in the trees reveal Wengen below and the surrounding mountain views.

> At this point you enter the forest of **avalanche protection**. Some are substantial metal structures, others solid wooden tripods. Boards explain how they work, and one claims the slope is 80°! Unless you have an iron grip on your sense of exposure, they will become your friends for the next hour or so.

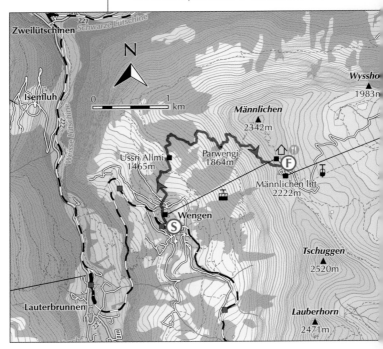

The route through the avalanche protection high on the Gemsweg

Climb steeply alongside and then into the protection. ▶ At around 2050m, a small path crosses, this heads more directly to the Männlichen summit. Continue ahead on the good path, for a while traversing open slopes outside the avalanche protection zone and under the cable car lines, before climbing to a gap between **Männlichen** cable car station and the restaurant and gondola lift (2222m, 3hr).

Looking down, it all looks much easier!

Amazingly the slopes here are harvested for hay and the crop taken down to the village.

WALK 28
Wengen and the Mendelssohn memorial

Start/Finish	Wengen station 1276m
Distance	5km
Total ascent	250m
Total descent	250m
Grade	1
Time	1hr 30min
Max altitude	1416m
Refreshments	Wengen
Access	Train from Lauterbrunnen or Kleine Scheidegg, cable car from Männlichen

This walk combines a visit to the Mendelssohn memorial, a delightful woodland walk, and an excursion to Wengwald which offers the very best viewpoint to look down the Lauterbrunnen valley towards the magnificent mountain peaks beyond. The return to the centre of Wengen follows an easy path rising just above the railway line.

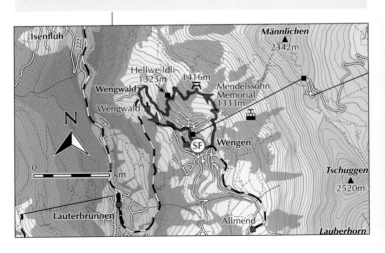

The Mendelssohn Memorial

From the station, walk out from the platform and take the small road rising parallel to the tracks up past the Hotel Regina and Falcon hotel, then at a road junction turn left and continue between chalets, signed in the direction of the swimming pool and Beausite Park.

Pass the swimming pool, then turn right up the track immediately before the Beausite Park Hotel then left onto a good path which climbs up through woods to reach the **Mendelssohn Memorial** at Mesti (Meschti in some spellings) 1333m, 1km, 20min.

The **Mendelssohn Memorial** is situated at the location where, on 21 August 1842, Mendelssohn drew a sketch of Wengen and the distant Jungfrau while on one of his alpine walks. The sketch is considered to be the oldest historical representation of Wengen. The view might have been slightly different for Mendelssohn, as currently there are one or two tall pine trees obscuring the view of the Jungfrau from this exact spot.

To continue the walk, the path continues in two more zigzags, then turn left onto a rising track to a point at 1416m, where there is a junction of two paths crossing the track, and a picnic area 1.5km, 35min.

Turn left onto the descending path, and on meeting a track turn right past woodpiles and descend round a hairpin left, then to the next hairpin bend where there are several forestry buildings at **Hellweidli**, 1323m, 2.5km, 50min. Continue just round this right-hand hairpin then immediately left down a pretty woodland path. ◄

If time is short, for a more direct route back to the centre of Wengen, take the track on the apex of the hairpin bend. This leads directly down, turning right and descending past the Palace Hotel then steeply down into the main street. This saves approximately 30min, and 2km.

Descend the woodland path to a small road and turn right to walk gently down with views ahead to the group of chalets that comprises **Wengwald** nestling in a bowl in the hillside. Just past chalet Der Lisabeth on a left-hand bend, take the delightful grassy path through fruit trees between chalets and gardens down to join a small road.

Views from this point down into the Lauterbrunnen valley are superb, with the impressive mountain wall from the Jungfrau right through to the Gletscherhorn, Mittaghorn, Grosshorn and Breithorn, and the Schilthorn above Mürren dominating the scene.

Ignoring the path ahead that leads to the main descent route to Lauterbrunnen, turn left onto the level track to enjoy the amazing views into the Lauterbrunnen valley, then at the tiny **Wengwald station**, take the path to the left that crosses the tracks. Climbing steeply with the tracks always just below and to the right, continue

climbing all the way up, following yellow footpath signs to reach the main street of **Wengen** 5km, 1hr 30min.

Wengwald has superb views of the Jungfrau and Lauterbrunnen valley

WALK 29

Wengen – Stalden – Allmend – Wengen

Start/Finish	Wengen station 1276m
Distance	10km
Total ascent	425m
Total descent	425m
Grade	2
Time	3hr
Max altitude	1695m
Refreshments	Wengen, Allmend
Access	Train from Lauterbrunnen or Kleine Scheidegg, cable car from Männlichen

This walk is a good choice on a hot day, as much of the time is spent in pine woods, keeping you cool and out of direct sun. While most of the walks from Wengen explore the hillside to the north, this route explores the hills to the south, while hugging close to the cliff line above the vast Lauterbrunnen valley. There are occasional clearings in the woods providing views down into the valley, and across to Mürren and the hillside opposite. The descent route on a gravel track is also mainly through woods until Allmend, where well-earned refreshments can be enjoyed with fine views.

From the **Wengen** train station, exit and turn right in front of the Hotel Silberhorn and descend passing under the railway line to reach a five-way junction. Take the second left signed to Stalden.

This minor road takes a roughly level balcony route, passing by houses and where paths fork, keep right on the road to **Innerwengen** (1.6km 20min).

The **chair lift** between Innerwengen and Allmend operates from July to the end of September 11:30–16:40. Service runs from Friday–Sunday from July to mid-August, and on Saturday and Sunday until the end of September. An easy weekend walk could begin in Wengen, using the chair lift to Allmend for refreshments, then a gentle walk back (or even the train if you are feeling really relaxed!).

Continue up the road then turn left signed to Stalden, then at **Schiltwald** (2km, 1310m), continue straight on, now on a gravel track signed to Stalden. Keep left at the next fork now on a path through pine woods. At the next fork take the left fork (although either path is fine as they join a little higher up). Cross a stream and climb steeply in zigzags.

The pine woods are beautiful, with occasional clearings through which the mountain landscape above Mürren can be seen. The path levels out after 3.8km, at a height of 1520m with a particularly good viewpoint just off the path to the right.

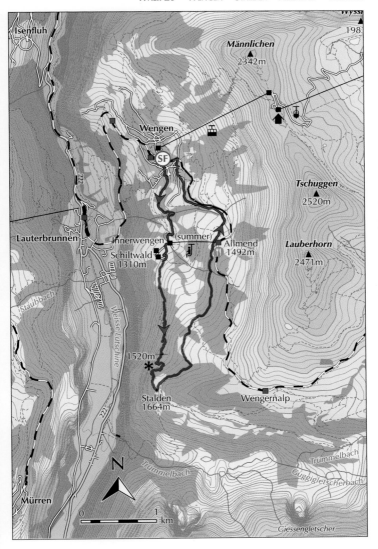

Mürren seen from a clearing near Stalden

After a brief level section, climb a little more in zig-zags to eventually emerge from the woods at **Stalden** (1664m, 5.0km, 1hr 45min) by a signpost. Turn left to Allmend on the rising path to join a gravel track and walk easily down through light pine woodland to **Allmend** 1492m. Refreshments, train stop.

From the restaurant, continue down the gravel track, then after 10min reach a metalled road, fork left and continue down following signs leading you into **Wengen** (9.8km, 3hr).

WALK 30

The Trümmelbach falls:
Wengen – Stalden – Trümmelbach

Start	Wengen 1274m
Finish	Trümmelbach falls 819m
Distance	10km
Total ascent	460m
Total descent	920m
Grade	3
Time	3hr 30min
Max altitude	1664m, Stalden
Refreshments	Wengen, then none until Trümmelbach falls
Access	Train from Lauterbrunnen or Kleine Scheidegg

The Trümmelbach falls are one of the must-see places in the Lauterbrunnen valley. From the visitor attraction (see Walk 34) the caverns of the numerous falls are an impressive sight. But how to approach the walk, either up or down the valley wall, is a question. Up is a fine hillwalking challenge, but this route starts at Wengen and climbs steadily through the wonderful woods to Stalden, before dropping down the steep descent to the falls. At times the valley seems so close underfoot you might think the cliffs are nearly vertical. Clearly this isn't quite the case, and the route makes a cunning descent to the valley floor with cables, a ladder, and a crossing of the upper part of the falls where they disappear into a canyon. All the while the glaciers of the Jungfrau and Mönch that feed the falls are high above, whilst the crashing falls are heard through the middle section of the descent.

From **Wengen** Bahnhof, pass under the railway and continue slightly downhill. Keep straight ahead where the Lauterbrunnen route heads downhill and continue straight ahead on the small road (Schiltwaldweg) initially through hotels and then chalets. Pass a deep indentation in woods where a stream descends, and then older chalets. Pass close under the lift to Allmend, and then up the

157

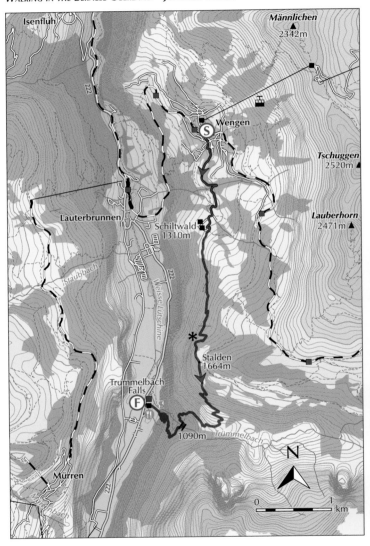

Isenfluh

Männlichen
2342m

Wengen

Tschuggen
2520m

Lauterbrunnen

Schiltwald
1310m

Lauberhorn
2471m

Staubbach

Weisse Lütschine

222

*

Stalden
1664m

Trummelbach
Falls

1090m

Trümmelbach

Mürren

222

N

0   1
|____|____|____|____| km

158

small road to the farm buildings at **Schiltwald** (1310m, 30min). The Stalden path is directly ahead.

Initially cross pastures and then into the woods. Although there are other paths, none are signed. The path is excellent, mainly climbing with steps. ▶ After the 1600m Staldenflue viewpoint, climb to the clearing at **Stalden** (1664m, 1hr 45min).

There are views across to Mürren and the Lauterbrunnen valley waterfalls.

Turn right on the Trümmelbach path. A sign warns that this is no place for cyclists, and it's hard to disagree. The path starts its long descent almost immediately, with a few cable sections early on. Pass into a large clearing with a farm building (Preech) at 1400m. ▶ Descend again through woods and pass another clearing (Trimmleten) at 1300m. Here you can hear the crashing of the Trümmelbach stream for the first time. Pass a rocky section, with cables and a ladder before resuming the descent.

From here you look directly up to the glaciers feeding the Trümmelbach torrent from the Mönch and Jungfrau and down to the valley floor seemingly directly below.

Looking back up the extra steep bottom section of the long, steep descent to Trümmelbach

Its suddenly cooler down here and it will be difficult to resist taking photos of the Trümmelbach as it disappears into a deep canyon on its way to the falls and the valley floor.

The noise of the stream fades as you tack north but gradually returns as you turn south and descend dropping steeply into the gorge created by the stream at a **bridge at 1090m**. Signs advise not spending too long on the bridge in case pieces of glacier create floods in the stream. ◄

Climb steeply for around 40m out of the ravine with many cables on a section that can stay wet year-round, passing a well-sited bench. Descend the path, which is increasingly steep. The last 150m of the descent are carved into the cliff and with protective cables the whole way down.

Cross fields and pass a house, turn right on the road to arrive at the **Trümmelbach falls attraction and restaurant** (819m, 3hr 30min). Buses leave for Lauterbrunnen every half hour.

LAUTERBRUNNEN
AND ISENFLUH

The Eiger looms over Kleine Scheidegg on the descent into Mürren (Walk 32)

WALK 31
Saxeten to Isenfluh

Start	Saxeten 1110m
Finish	Isenfluh 1090m
Distance	14km
Total ascent	980m
Total descent	1000m
Grade	2–3 (Grade 3 only for the traverse of Tschingel)
Time	5hr 15min
Max altitude	2050m on the shoulder of the Tschingel
Refreshments	Saxeten, possible refreshments at high farm in summer, Lobhornhütte, Sulwald and Isenfluh
Access	Train from Lauterbrunnen to Wilderswil, then bus to Saxeten (Schulhaus stop). Return by Sulwald lift and bus from Isenfluh to Lauterbrunnen

This longish route from the village of Saxeten above Interlaken uses Swiss Route 38, the ViaBerna to emerge into the Mürren region. It is easily reached from Mürren, explores a quiet side-valley, crosses a low col, makes a rather dramatic traverse of a vast mountain combe before reaching the welcoming Lobhornhütte and dropping down to transport links. The last hour can be avoided by using the Sulwald lift.

It's fine walking country. The only word of warning is that if there is a lot of snow on the Tschingel, then it would be better to avoid the route (or return to the valley) unless you are fully equipped to deal with it.

Take the train to Wilderswil and bus from the station to Saxeten Schulhaus. From **Saxeten** Schulhaus head down the hill and turn right across the bridge. Head steadily up the beautiful track alongside the Saxetbach steam. Come to a junction at a hairpin at **1200m**, 25min.

Turn left at the hairpin and the path immediately becomes a narrower ascending path, mainly through woods with glimpses of the valley and then

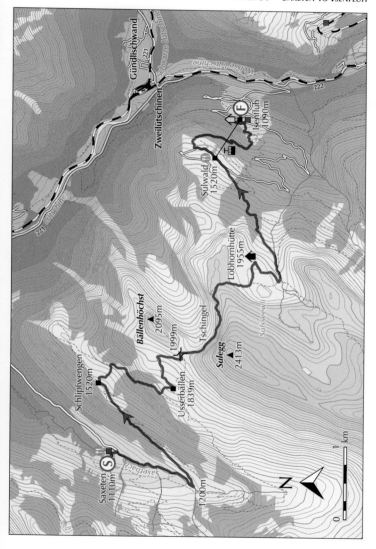

Saxeten increasingly far below. Cross a climbing service road three times, passing a small lift servicing the higher pastures. Come to a substantial farm building at **Schlipfwengen** (1520m, 1hr 25min).

THE VIABERNA

This 305km Swiss regional route takes a meandering path through the Bern Canton starting in the Jura, passing Biel, Bern itself and then to Spiez. The appetising mountain section of the route has stages to Saxeten, Schynige Platte, First, Rosenlaui, Reuti, Engstlenalp, Gadmen and finishes on the Susten Pass.

Turn right and pass through the farm. Traverse above the farm, but soon the path bends left and climbs steeply up the hillside. Join another path and head right under sheer cliffs on a good path, with steps that are rather too big for short legs. Turn left at a junction at 1796m, and climb to high farm buildings at **Usserbällen** (1839m), where there is a possibility of refreshments.

Turn left along a concrete and likely cow-pat covered path, and bend right at higher barns. Follow the rutted path to the **col at 1999m** (2hr 40min). The col separates the sheerly rising **Sulegg** at 2413m looming above and the 2095m **Bällehöchst**, a grassy knoll on the left which is a fine viewpoint up towards Grindelwald and down towards Interlaken and the Breinzersee. ◄

It is a 30m round trip to climb Bällehöchst.

Ahead is the path traversing the valley headwall under the **Tschingel rocks**. The appearance is most dramatic, but the path is very good under summer conditions. But if snow is covering the path or the hillside then unless you are experienced and have appropriate axe, crampons and know how to use them, then it would be better to return by the route climbed.

Drop down 25m and start the traverse. It takes around 30min to make the crossing and the steeper sections are

on the far side. There is limited protection (some rather tired barbed wire at present), but little is needed. Climb to the saddle on the far side at 2050m.

Continue steadily down. The **Sulsseewli** tarn comes into view but before reaching it find a sign to the **Lobhornhütte** (1955m) and turn left arriving at the hut after 3hr 30min.

From the hut follow the path down through a narrow limestone alley to the Suls dairy (cheese available to purchase). Turn left and head down the good path initially in the open but soon in woods. Although it is a good path, there are steps that seem just a bit too big. Eventually emerge in pastures and then a road; turn left for **Sulwald** (1520m, 4hr 25min). Refreshments and cable car to Isenfluh.

To walk to Isenfluh 430m below, continue past the cable car and after 400m take a path descending pastures. The path is a little indistinct at first, but at the bottom of the pastures it becomes clear again. Follow into woods, a short distance on a track before turning right and descending. ▶ Drop down through woods on a

The last part of the traverse climbs through a series of coves to emerge on a grassy saddle

There may be forestry operations in the area so look out for warning signs and possible re-routing.

rather rough path. At around 1280m, come into a clearing and head down through pastures to a track and turn left. After 200m turn right and follow the signs for a somewhat intricate descent into **Isenfluh** (1090m, 5hr 15min).

WALK 32
Sulwald to Mürren by the Lobhorn Hut

Start	Sulwald 1520m
Finish	Mürren 1638m
Distance	14km
Total ascent	920m
Total descent	800m
Grade	2
Time	5hr 15min
Max altitude	1955m at the Lobhornhütte
Refreshments	Sulwald, then at the Lobhornhütte after 1hr 15min and Allmendhubel towards the end of the route (after nearly 5hr), Mürren
Access	Bus from Lauterbrunnen to Isenfluh, then the lift to Sulwald

The Lobhornhütte is blessed with spectacular views of the Oberland Giants and makes a popular destination for walkers using the convenient buses to Isenfluh and the 8-person unmanned gondola lift to Sulwald. Both Isenfluh and Sulwald have much to explore and several routes in this guide converge on them. From the Lobhorn hut back to Mürren is a high-level traverse at around 1800m with simply stunning views of Eiger, Mönch and Jungfrau throughout. One of the best walks in the region.

If walking from Isenfluh add 1hr and 435m of height gain.

Buses to Isenfluh leave from Lauterbrunnen station, then take the cable car to Sulwald. From the small lift station (and bar) turn left and walk up the road. ◀ The route follows Swiss Route 38 used in Walk 31 (the ViaBerna, a 305km 20-stage meandering tour of Bern Canton). After

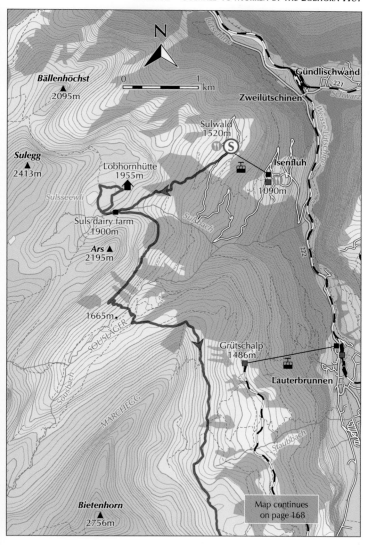

Map continues
on page 168

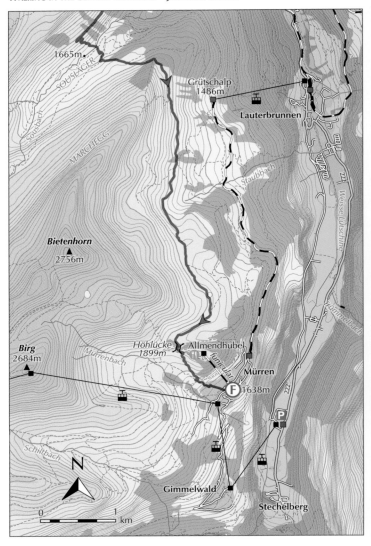

1665m.

SOUSLAGER

MARCHEGG

Grütschalp
1486m

Lauterbrunnen

Staubbach

Weisse Lütschine

Bietenhorn
▲
2756m

Höhlücke
1899m ▲ Allmendhubel

Birg
2684m
▲ ■

Mürrenbach

funicular

Mürren

F 1638m

222

Schiltbach

P

N

0   1 km

Gimmelwald ■

Stechelberg

Zumbbach

400m, the road heads down and the path heads up. Climb in woods, sometimes steeply, on a well-made path. Pass two paths on the left that are signed to Grütschalp, and after 1hr emerge at the **Suls dairy farm** at 1900m (cheese for sale). Take a path right (still on Route 38) and climb through a limestone alley, arriving at the **Lobhornhütte** (1955m, 1hr 15min).

> The **situation** is magnificent, the Eiger, Mönch and Jungfrau across the valley dominate the view whilst the pointed Lobhorner rises above. This is fine walking country, and the hut makes for a memorable overnight stay, although facilities are limited (and outside).

Head back 10m and then west away from the hut to find the **Sulsseewli** tarn, attractive in its limestone surroundings. Take the path left and drop down to the Suls farm buildings. Continue down the Sulsbach stream for 300 metres (on the path used on the way up) and turn right across a bridge, signed to Grütschalp.

Eiger Mönch and Jungfrau, seen from the Mountain View Trail

Cross open hillsides with dramatic views interspersed with shaded woods.

The path contours round the bulky buttress of the **Ars**. The general trend is down, but barely noticeably with a few kicks upwards. ◀ After 2hr 30min the path takes a sharp left turn and drops steeply for some 120m to the valley floor at **Sousläger** (1665m, 2hr 40min).

A path is signed for Grütschalp, take this if you want or need to shorten the walk by around 1hr 30min.

Cross the steam and climb the hillside directly ahead. Follow the path first left and then right into an open area. ◀ Our path to the right heads steeply up amongst small trees round the Marchegg ridge of the Soushorn. At the top of the climb (around 1850m), remarkable close-up views of the Jungfrau peaks dominate everything, a bench has been placed there to allow time for admiration (and/or a rest). Continue along the traversing path which gradually descends, in the presence of these sublime views. Come to a junction with Route 351 (1768m, 3hr 40min) which has climbed from Grütschalp (see Walk 36). ◀

This path is well named as the 'Mountain View Trail'.

Continue ahead, traversing, with short climbs and descents. After crossing a low ridge, the path drops to join a track (still the 351). Continue ahead, the buildings of Allmendhubel are now visible. Drop down 50m then climb back steeply to arrive at the **Höhlücke saddle** (1899m, 4hr 50min).

There are several options at this point to **finish the trail**. Left takes you to the Allmendhubel funicular station with refreshments and a quick descent to Mürren. A descending path to the right leads to the mountain inns at Sonnenberg and Suppenalp with easy paths and farm lanes into Mürren adding 15min walking to the day. Or continue directly down to Mürren as described.

Continue straight ahead. After 2min cross a track but continue down on the steep path, eroded in places and repaired in others. Come to a road by a fine new barn building named 'Mürren Beef'. Turn left on a gravel track which becomes a paved road and emerges in the centre of **Mürren** (1638m, 5hr 15min).

WALK 33
Grütschalp to Sulwald and onward routes

Start	Grütschalp 1486m
Finish	Sulwald 1520m
Distance	6.5km
Total ascent	400m
Total descent	360m
Grade	2
Time	2hr 20min
Max altitude	1713m near Souslager
Refreshments	Grütschalp and Sulwald only, none on the route
Access	Train from Mürren to Grütschalp, or funicular from Lauterbrunnen. Descent from Sulwald by cable car and from Isenfluh by bus

This mainly level walk connects the station at Grütschalp with the fine walking country to the north and west around Sulwald and Isenfluh, quiet hamlets with restaurants and outstanding views. Traversing mainly in woods on good paths, there are views at first to the Eiger, and later to the hills above and behind Grindelwald.

Leave Grütschalp station by a step directly from the upper viewing area. Turn right, then immediately left onto a path into meadows and take the second path to the right. The lower path may be used as a return route from Isenfluh (see below), the higher also leads to Sousläger. Soon head into woods with glimpses of the Eiger and Wengen across the valley. The path ascends gradually until a junction with an ascending path at a **1542m path junction** after 35min.

Continue on the path which now rises steadily over the course of 1.5km. The path steadily turns the corner of the **Marchegg** ridge above with views across to Sulwald and Isenfluh across the valley. Meet a track and follow

Approaching the gondola and café at Sulwald

the path left into an area of lumpy open pasture, and 2min later find one of Switzerland's most complex path signs. **Sousläger** 1682m, 1hr 10min.

Turn right directly downhill to the stream below. Cross the walkers' bridge and follow a path right signed to Sulwald. Climb briefly and come to a short, protected descent section. The path is now in woods, then crossing open hillsides with views across to the Schynige Platte–Faulhorn range across the valley. Pass an open pasture with barns dotted around and climb to **Chüebodmi** (1713m, 2hr), where we join with Rt 38 path descending from the Lobhorn hut to Sulwald (see Walk 31).

Turn right and follow the good path (albeit with some large steps to descend). Cross a track and continue down, coming into meadows and houses. Turn left on the road and come to **Sulwald cable car station** (and bar) 1520m, after 2hr 20min.

Options from Sulwald
Onward options include taking the unmanned cable car down to Isenfluh, or walking down the steep path in 50min (see Walk 31). It would also be practicable to walk to the **Lobhorn Hut** in 1hr 15min from Sulwald.

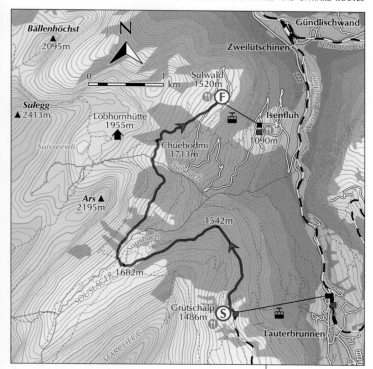

From Isenfluh there are several options:
- Walk back to **Grütschalp** by a lower route. Walk up the track from the cable car, turn sharply left and follow the minor metalled road through woods, cross the Sulsbach and Sousbach streams and climb to 1299m. Descend past a works area then take the path to the right up through beautiful woods then climb two big zigzags to **Grütschalp**.
- Descending to **Lauterbrunnen** on a good quiet traffic-free back lane in 40min.
- Taking one of the hourly buses down to **Lauterbrunnen**.

WALK 34

Lauterbrunnen, Trümmelbach falls and Stechelberg

Start	Lauterbrunnen train station 797m
Finish	Rütti bus terminus (Stechelberg Hotel) 910m
Distance	7.5km
Total ascent	150m
Total descent	40m
Grade	1
Time	2hr
Max altitude	910m Rütti
Refreshments	Trümmelbach, Stechelberg, Rütti
Access	Train at Lauterbrunnen, bus at all points in the valley

Walking up the Lütschine valley is an awe-inspiring experience. This deep 'U' shaped valley was carved by huge glaciers and is a great, yet very easy walk on any day. The Lauterbrunnen valley is known for its superb waterfalls, which are at their best in spring and early summer as the snow melts; while on wet days, although the higher mountains might be mostly obscured, the waterfalls are amazing at any time of year. The Trümmelbach falls are impressive, and you should allow at least an hour to view the falls. The settlements at Stechelberg and Rütti at the head of the main valley provide a starting point to explore the Upper Lauterbrunnen valley within the Untersteinberg UNESCO world heritage protected nature reserve (see Walks 47, 48, 49 and 50).

It's possible to walk up to, and behind the falls for a closer look.

From the station, walk up the ramp and onto the main street through Lauterbrunnen. Keep on the road ahead and shortly after leaving the village the impressive Staubbach falls can be seen on the right. ◀

The **Staubbach falls** are 297m high, cascading in a single drop. The height was first measured successfully in 1776 when Johan Samuel dropped rope the entire length of the falls, then measured it, the

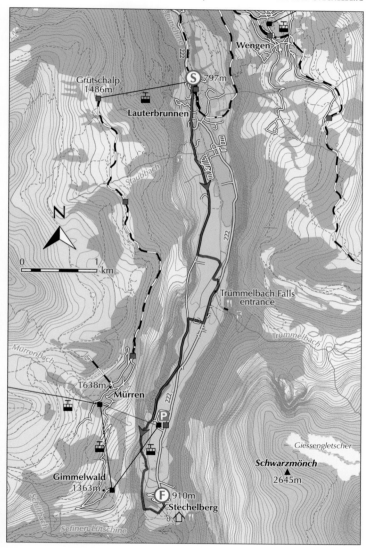

length recorded as 900 Berne shoes (feet), or 816 'King's shoes'.

Allow at least an hour for your visit, the falls are on several levels and are very impressive.

After viewing the falls continue up the valley and after 2.6km take the path left by a tree, signed to Trümmelbach, cross the Lütschine, then shortly after cross the Trümmelbach to reach the entrance to the **Trümmelbach Falls** (3.4km, 45min). ◄

THE TRÜMMELBACH FALLS

Inside the Trümmelbach falls

The falls are Europe's largest subterranean falls, carrying up to 20,000 litres per second of glacial meltwater from the glaciers above the Eiger, Mönch and Jungfrau, in a series of ten corkscrewing cascades. Accessed by an underground funicular, the upper cascades are reached by a series of stairs and tunnels with lighting where needed, with numerous viewing balconies and openings, the falls and carved canyons illuminated wherever needed. The thundering of the water only begins to suggest its awesome power, while the sinuous carving of fantastic shapes into the rock provides amazing photo opportunities.

Leave the falls and turn left to continue up the valley, then turn right after 500 metres (7min), passing through a campsite, then turn left and continue on a riverside path, and through a lightly wooded area.

After a further 1.5km pass a track that crosses the river leading to the **cable car station** for Mürren and the Schilthorn, but ignore this and continue on the path straight ahead. The path briefly becomes metalled. Ignore a sign to Stechelberg Post on the left, continue straight on to Rütti. The path leads over a substantial curved bridge next to some works buildings, past chalets and the Alpenhof (B&B accommodation), then left over a bridge and down to the bus stop just beyond the **Stechelberg** Hotel (910m) 7.5km, 2hr.

WALK 35

Lauterbrunnen to Mürren on the Via Alpina

Start	Lauterbrunnen 797m
Finish	Mürren 1638m
Distance	6.5km
Total ascent	850m
Total descent	10m
Grade	2
Time	2hr 45min
Max altitude	1638m at Mürren
Refreshments	The Winteregg station off the main route, Mürren
Access	Train to Lauterbrunnen. From Mürren take train to Grütschalp and cable car to Lauterbrunnen

The old mule track from Lauterbrunnen up to Mürren has been used for centuries and is a good path, well-graded and now carries the Swiss Route 1, Via Alpina route through the valley. By joining this with Walks 14, 19 and 45, a full traverse from Meiringen to Griesalp in the adjoining Kiental can be made over 4 days.

But why walk up 800m when there are good lifts available? It's a fine walk on a good path and allows time to look out for the deer and other wildlife in the forest, to inspect Wengen and the Jungfrau across the valley at close quarters. It's a good walk, and you are on a walking holiday, when all is said and done.

From **Lauterbrunnen** Bahnhof (where Walk 19 from Grindelwald finishes) walk up the main street for 400 metres and find the signs to the right for Route 1, also signed for the Police and *Schwimmenbad*. Head between houses up the lane and after 5min, meet another path from Lauterbrunnen Dorf (village) an alternative start point if preferred.

Head uphill, now steeply. Pass water control and a small generation facility and head into woods,

The Jungfrau and steep valley walls from early in the trail

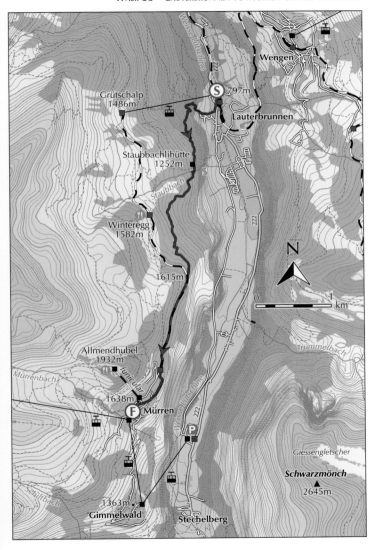

providing welcome shade on a hot day. The path heads north around steep drops and then turns south above the rocks that dominate the valley. A right turn heads up to Grütschalp but keep left and climb steadily, pass a couple of huts and cross streams. Climb steadily and come to the **Staubbachlihütte** (1252m, 1hr 10min), a shelter and bench around the halfway point in the climb, and soon after cross the Staubbach stream, which is surprisingly small given the vast 300m waterfall it becomes.

Continue the climb, seemingly more steadily now. Come into an open area with good views across to Wengen and beyond. Continue through this open area but look out for any diversion signs headed up and to the right (see below) as you enter woods.

Continue on the path, passing an area where there has been a landslide. The path has been reconstructed in 2022, but it's not impossible that there could be further regular work required as forestry clearance above has likely weakened the stability of the hillside.

Views here include the elusive Tschingelgletscher and Tschingelpass to Kandersteg 2–3 days' walk away.

Continue the climb and come to the railway track (1615m, 2hr 15min). ◄ Cross and take the seemingly level path that sits just above the track for around 2km into **Mürren** (1638m, 2hr 45min).

ROUTE DIVERSION TO WINTEREGG

As mentioned there has been construction work during 2022 and the path reopened in August 2022. If the work needs repeating, or indeed if you need refreshments before Mürren, then this diversion will satisfy either need, or both. At around 1390m as the path re-enters woods, find a good if unsigned path headed right and up. Follow this as it climbs and passes 2 barns. Find the continuing path across the Winteregg service road and take this, cross the road again and soon emerge at the **Winteregg station** 1582m (refreshments and an exceptionally fine view).

From Winteregg there are several options: take the train for 5min to Mürren; take a path close to the line or rejoin the Via Alpina 1 by dropping down past the café and play area and meeting the main route after 10min.

The diversion adds 200m of uphill and 100m of down (making it a 1000m ascent) and around 30min to the route.

MÜRREN

Looking along the arête to the Schilthorn (Walk 39)

WALK 36
The Mountain View Trail to Grütschalp

Start	Allmendhubel 1907m
Finish	Grütschalp 1486m
Alternative finish	Mürren 1638m
Distance	5.5km
Total ascent	110m
Total descent	530m
Grade	2
Time	1hr 45min
Max altitude	1910m
Refreshments	Allmendhubel, none on route. Limited at Grütschalp, Winteregg and Mürren if using alternative finish
Access	Funicular from Mürren
Note	This route can be walked in either direction, as the views are equally impressive, however if starting at Grütschalp the initial steep ascent is energy sapping on a hot day

Known as the mountain view trail, this is a popular traversing route high above the Lauterbrunnen valley, with impressive views of the Eiger, Mönch, Jungfrau and multiple peaks to the west, as well as views across to Wengen, with Männlichen above, and Schynige Platte in the distance.

Using mainly paths, much of the route crosses grassy pastures. The path descends steeply for the final 300m through pine woods to emerge at Grütschalp, for a return to Mürren by train, or descent to Lauterbrunnen by cable car.

An additional route from Grütschalp back to Mürren is briefly described below and will add a further 190m of ascent, 5km, 1hr 30min.

Emerging from the **Allmendhubel** funicular, walk up through the 'Flower Trail' arch then turn right onto a rising path. Information points describe various alpine flowers and aspects of the mountain flora and pasture management. Descend to a path junction at **Höhlücke** in 10min. (Named on sign, on maps).

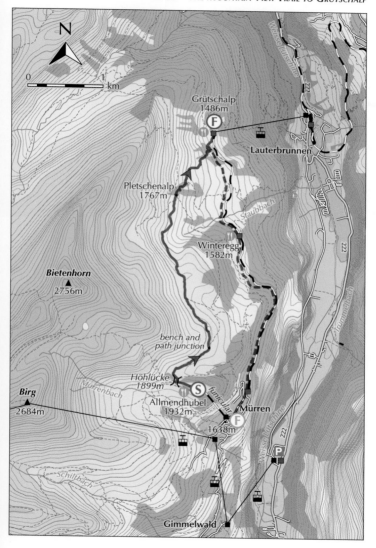

The Schwarzmönch (Black Monk) in front of the Jungfrau, with the Gletscherhorn, Mittaghorn and Grosshorn visible

Steep slopes high on your left ahead are covered with avalanche defences.

Turn right. The track descends steeply. Cross the Ägertenbach stream, continue ahead then climb to a grassy shoulder with a well-placed bench. 20min.

Views now stretch from Schynige Platte in a huge panorama to beyond the Breithorn. It is possibly the best place on the entire route to enjoy the magnificent scene.

Branch left away from the track onto a gently rising path across the hillside and soon reach a high point with a new view opening up briefly, to see Wengen perched on the hillside opposite. ◄

The long gently descending path skirts the pastures to eventually reach a path junction at **Pletschenalp** (1767m, 3.6km, 1hr 30min). Continue ahead then immediately fork right to begin the steep descent.

The path remains steep nearly all the way, passing through the lightly wooded hillside, past an alp building and down to join a track. Turn left then almost immediately fork left onto a path at a hairpin bend.

Good views on this open hillside are straight across to Wengen, then descend steeply across meadows and through more woods, turn left onto a track with the railway line seen below, and continue for a few more minutes to arrive at **Grütschalp** 1486m.

To walk back to Mürren
Take the track rising away from the railway line across pasture then enter woods, ignoring the path signed off to the right. The path rises steadily across more pastures, then keep left of a large alp building at 1559m and continue now almost level through more woods to **Winteregg** (1582m, 40min). From here an easy track keeps just above the railway tracks all the way to Mürren.

WALK 37
Mürren, the Blumental and Chänelegg

Start/Finish	Mürren 1638m
Distance	6km
Total ascent	335m
Total descent	335m
Grade	1–2
Time	2hr
Max altitude	1899m
Refreshments	Mürren, Suppenalp, Sonnenberg, Allmendhubel station (off route)
Access	Cable car/train from Lauterbrunnen valley

This is a lovely walk to explore the great grassy bowl of the Blumental valley and then to enter the Chänelegg protected area, enjoying superb views across the Lauterbrunnen valley towards the major peaks, and deep into the valley near where the Trümmelbach falls drop to the valley floor. The route climbs steeply to Suppenalp before crossing the Blumental. Continuing to Allmiboden, a good path then climbs through beautiful, protected woodland to 1833m, with tremendous views. The descent via Mittelberg is at a steady gradient, but watch out for tree roots!

From the signpost in Mürren just to the south of the Co-op supermarket, take Bachstutz street, then the left-hand forking lane that rises past chalets indicated by yellow Wanderweg signs. The path crosses the Mürrenbach stream to reach a path junction with a playground ahead, 8min. Turn right and begin the fairly steep climb up a path with the stream now on your right, passing two chalets where the gradient eases and briefly join a track. ◄ At the next junction of tracks turn left signed to Im Suppen, pass to the left of a large works building, then climb again on a fairly steep path to reach **Suppenalp** 40min (refreshments, closed Monday and Tuesday).

The intermittent hum of the Schilthorn cable car and cowbells only mildly disturb the peaceful scene.

Continue beyond Suppenalp on a gravel track which curves gradually to the right as it crosses the wide bowl of the Blumental – an area rich in pasture, with the rocky

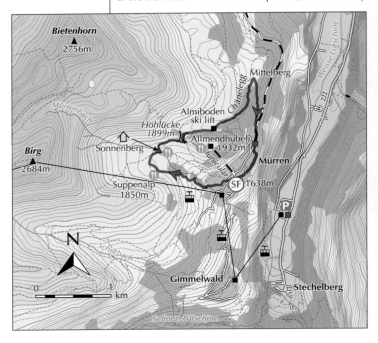

186

Walkers descending into the Blumental basin, with the rocky outcrop of Birg seen above

buttress of Birg and beyond that the Schilthorn towering above. Ahead is the **Sonnenberg hotel/restaurant** 50min (refreshments). Just before reaching the Sonnenberg hotel take the track forking to the left and climb easily up the side of the hillside, then take the track rising sharply to the left signed to the Schilthorn and Schilthorn hut, to reach a small saddle at 1899m (**Höhlücke**, 2.7km, 1hr). ▶

Drop steeply part way down then fork right onto a path that heads down directly towards the **Allmiboden/ Maulerhubel ski lift station**. At a junction with a track turn left towards the ski lift, then right in front of the building onto a woodland path. You are now entering the **Chänelegg** protected area.

The **Chänelegg** protected area covers nearly 4.5 hectares (11 acres), consisting of woodland and moorland undisturbed by farming or winter sports activities. The area lies above a line of cliffs which run in a north-south direction between Allmiboden and Mittelberg, however you are never obviously near the cliff edge.

For refreshments and the funicular at Allmendhubel, turn right past exhibits of alpine flowers to reach Allmendhubel 5min.

The path climbs steadily through a beautiful area of light pine woods, with juniper, bilberries, alpenrose and heather all competing with a variety of wildflowers. As height is gained views open up, until a broad grassy area is reached at the highpoint of 1833m, with great views across the valley to the mountain wall opposite, and deep into the valley below.

From here, continue on the path now descending steadily through more woods (with numerous tree roots to dodge), to come to a clearing and path junction at **Mittelberg** 4.5km, 1hr 45min. ◀ Turn right onto the path signed to Mürren and continue your descent, to meet the road next to the railway just to the north of the **Mürren** station. To continue into the village centre, walk past the station and along the main street to the centre of the village.

Views are now also across towards Wengen, Männlichen and Schynige Platte beyond.

WALK 38
The North Face Trail – Allmendhubel to Mürren via Schiltalp

Start	Allmendhubel 1907m
Finish	Mürren 1638m
Distance	6.5km
Total ascent	180m
Total descent	450m
Grade	1–2
Time	2hr 10min
Max altitude	1958m
Refreshments	Allmendhubel, Sonnenberg, Suppenalp, Schiltalp, Spielbodenalp, Mürren
Access	Funicular from Mürren
Note	Most of the alpine restaurants are closed on Monday, some also on Tuesday. Schiltalp is self-service and open every day

This is a superb route enjoying constant dramatic views across the Lauterbrunnen valley to the huge mountain wall opposite, as well as to Birg and the Schilthorn above. There is the added benefit that the route is sprinkled with a generous number of mountain pensions and restaurants, providing opportunities to sit and admire the superb views.

The route has information boards occasionally sited to draw attention to particular mountains and the most notable ascents made on them. There is little difficulty either in terrain or route finding.

From the funicular station at **Allmendhubel**, walk out and take the track ahead to the left passing the giant Allmendhubel sign, and follow this broad gravel track descending round the hillside with views to the high mountains and up to Birg and the Schilthorn. Keep straight on past a crossing path then after 15min reach a junction just before the **Sonnenberg hotel** (refreshments). Turn right, then fork left.

The track leads easily round to **Suppenalp** 1850m (refreshments). Pass in front of the building with its sunny

Ceremonial cowbells proudly on display at Schiltalp

Information boards
sponsored by the
North Face focus
on mountaineering
ascents of most
of the main peaks
seen on the
opposite side of the
Lauterbrunnen valley.

terrace, then take the rising path ahead marked with red/white paint splashes. (The path left descends directly to Mürren.) Climb steadily, curving around the hillside and occasionally in light woodland passing under two sets of cable car lines. ◄ After reaching a high point the path descends to the Alp buildings at **Schiltalp** 1946m, 2.7km, 1hr (self-serve refreshments, cheese for sale).

Turn left to head downhill on a track, then at the next junction take the path to the right signed Spielboden. Be careful to take the path, not the track at this point. The path heads fairly steeply downhill to the Schiltbach stream. Cross over on a wooden bridge then continue to **Spielbodenalp** (1793m, 4km, 1hr 25min, refreshments).

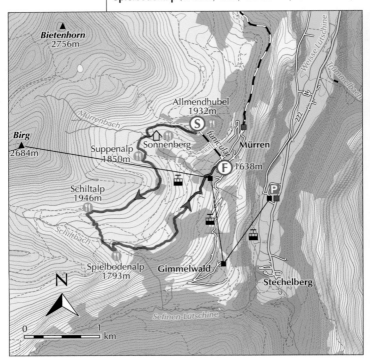

To continue, take the descending path to re-cross the Schiltbach stream, then continue on the slightly rising path past a chalet then enter the edge of woods, now descending gently. Emerge into meadows with views ahead directly down towards Mürren, and ahead to the Klein Scheidegg, with the Eiger rising impressively above to the right.

Pass through more woods and meadows to join the main road leading down to **Mürren** to arrive next to the Schilthorn cable car station (2hr 10min). To continue into town, proceed along the main street.

Jungfrau and mountain wall to the south seen from near Schiltalp

191

WALK 39

The 'easy' way up the Schilthorn
from Allmendhubel

Start	Allmendhubel 1907m
Finish	Schilthorn 2970m
Distance	6.5km
Total ascent	1085m
Total descent	25m
Grade	3
Time	3hr 30min
Max altitude	Schilthorn at 2970m
Refreshments	Allmendhubel, Schilthornhütte after 1hr 30min, Birg (30min off route), the Schilthorn station
Access	Take the Allmendhubel funicular from central Mürren

This is probably the easiest route up the Schilthorn, on foot anyway. It's a half-day walk if you use the cable car in descent. The first third is a stern ascent, the second is a gently ascending track and the last is a stiff climb up to the summit with a couple of narrow passages well protected by cable. The views are stunning, the tourists may be surprised to see you emerge at the top, but they are paying for the infrastructure for your trip down so appreciate their enjoyment.

The summit is steep and if you find it under snow or other poor conditions it would be better to leave it for another trip unless you are equipped and confident using mountaineering gear – crampons and ice axe.

From here paths head left to Suppenalp and right on the high trail to Grütschalp.

Views back to the Eiger and Jungfrau can help distract from the unrelenting slope.

From **Allmendhubel** take the path past the Flower Garden, and in under 10min, drop down to the **Höhlücke** (1899m). ◄

Continue straight ahead on the path/piste that climbs very steeply through the narrow gap between buttresses. This ski descent through the narrow cleft is referred to as Kanonenrohr (the gun barrel). At the steepest point a path snakes more easily on the right of the track. ◄ Follow the line of a chairlift and as you pass under it (around

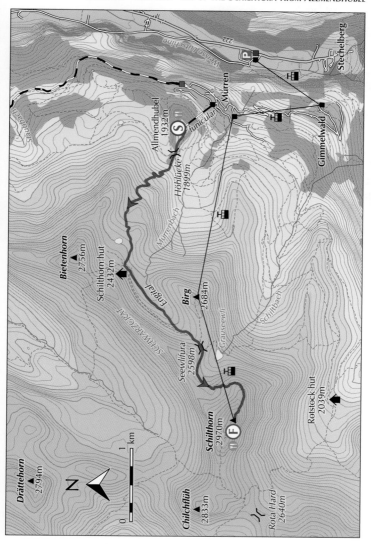

The Grauseewli tarn with Jungfrau behind

It has been closed some summers, so check ahead if you plan to rely on the hut for refreshments.

2420m), take a rough path straight ahead as the track veers right. 10min later come to a path junction. The **Schilthornhütte** (2432m, 1hr 30min) is just to the left. ◀

Continue along a track gradually climbing the hemmed-in **Engital**. The rocks of the Schwarzgrat are above on the right, the Birg cable car station is perched on rocks to the left, not hugely attractive, it must be admitted. And ahead is the triangular form of the Schilthorn, the top station perched right on the summit. After 2hr come to a junction, keep right and cross the broad col – the **Seewlifura** (2598m, 2hr) and to a fine viewpoint above the attractive Grauseewli, nearly 100m below.

The path ahead is clearly signed (almost excessively so, but the markings are welcome).

Contour right on a good path, the Schilthorn looming above. Even in a warm summer, there may be some snow accumulating at the foot of the rocks. ◀ Climb through a narrow rock band to the left. The path then opens and climbs steeply before joining the narrow ridge of the Chlys Schilthoren. A narrow set of steps carved into the rock, with cable supports, is followed by a narrow ridge dropping a little to the summit climb. If you miss the steps, there is a lower but not necessarily easier path.

From the point where the ridge joins the upper mountain is a stiff climb to the top. Arrive at the **Schilthorn summit** (2970m, 3hr 30min).

THE SCHILTHORN

Originally opened in 1967 and a major attraction for visitors to the Lauterbrunnen valley and Mürren ever since, the station's revolving restaurant is referred to as Piz Gloria and has 360° panoramic views covering the central part of the Bernese range from Wetterhorn to Gspaltenhorn and overlooks the lower valleys.

The station has long traded on its James Bond connections from the film *On Her Majesty's Secret Service* with extracts from the film and whole screenings available and information about the creation of the film sequences that involved many locals and guides (often as James's enemies – Blofeld's nasty crew).

Arrival at the station is a somewhat bizarre experience with tourists from across the globe mingling with the stalwart walkers who have made their way up. But accept with grace the lift down and enjoy the stunning views.

Options on the ascent

If you intend to climb to Birg, add 25min from the Seewlifura turn, 45min round trip.

If you wanted to take the cable car to Birg and climb the Schilthorn, allow 1hr 30min for the 2.5km, 400m ascent. From the Birg station take the service track down 100m to the Seewlifura and follow the route described.

WALK 40
The Schilthorn via Schiltalp and Grauseewli

Start	Mürren 1638m
Finish	Schilthorn 2970m
Distance	8km
Total ascent	1360m
Total descent	30m
Grade	3
Time	4hr
Max altitude	2970m at the top of the Schilthorn
Refreshments	Mürren, Spielbodenalp, Schiltalp and the Schilthorn summit

This route tackles the quieter side of the Schilthorn, joining with the Schilthornhütte route only for the final 350m up the mountain. The lower section passes alps providing refreshments, then there is a stern climb to the attractive Grauseewli lake before the steep final climb to the Schilthorn summit. It's slightly longer than the normal route (Walk 39) but a quieter and arguably better route.

Leave the centre of **Mürren** in the direction of the Schilthornbahn. Keep to Swiss Route 1, passing under the lift's cables and then climbing on the farm lane. Look out for a left turn after 15min, and follow the path, crossing streams and passing several woods and gates, to arrive at **Spielbodenalp** (1791m, 45min, refreshments).

The Bryndli/Wasenegg alternative
From Spielbodenalp, follow signs to the Rotstock hut, climb the steep Bryndli spur. 200 metres after the route levels out, take a path climbing steeply uphill. It's possible to visit the summit of Bryndli. Continue on the **Wasenegg** ridge passing the Chlyni (lower) and Grossi (higher) Nadla. Follow the route round the upper Schilttal to meet the main route at **Tischtelwang** (2315m).

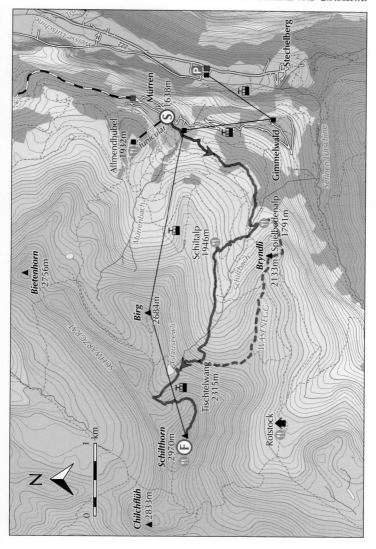

Looking back down the protected and fairly wide arête

Main route

Turn right at Spielbodenalp and head upstream signed to Schiltalp/Im Schilt. Cross the Schilt Bach on a bridge (or if dry, just cross the stream). ◄ Climb steadily to the farm buildings, turn left on a track at 1875m, and soon arrive at **Schiltalp** (1946m, 1hr 15min, self-service refreshments, cheese for sale).

An alternative ascent avoiding Schiltalp keeps left here.

Pass through the farm buildings and continue on a level track for around 1km. The route is playing games with you here, you soon meet the real work. Path reconstruction here should be completed in 2022, if there are continued detours, follow the waymarkings down and below them.

The route starts to climb, gradually at first but becoming steeper and steeper as the path climbs a grassy buttress between streams, with a sizeable ravine to the left. The path is good and stays good throughout. Climb to a path junction meeting the path from Bryndli/Wasenegg at **Tischtelwang** (2315m, 2hr 20min).

Continue upwards. There is a short section of chains protecting outward sloping rocks, but then the path is straightforward all the way to the **Grauseewli lake** (2514m, 2hr 45min) in a beautiful settling under the Schilthorn.

For the Schilthorn take the path to the left. (Right heads towards Birg, although it's possible to rejoin the route described taking 15min longer). In 15min arrive at the foot of the Schilthorn summit pyramid at 2614m.

▸ Climb through a narrow rock band to the left. The path then opens and climbs steeply before joining the narrow ridge of the Chlys Schilthoren. A narrow set of steps carved into the rock, with cable supports, is followed by a narrow ridge dropping a little to the summit climb. ▸ From the point where the ridge joins the upper mountain is a stiff climb to the top. Arrive at the **Schilthorn summit** 2970m, 4hr.

For details of the summit station and its James Bond connections, see Walk 39.

The path ahead is clearly signed (almost excessively so, but the markings are welcome).

If you miss the steps, there is a lower but not necessarily easier path.

WALK 41
Mürren – Gimmelwald – Mürren

Start/Finish	Mürren 1638m
Distance	5km
Total ascent	300m
Total descent	300m
Grade	1–2
Time	1hr 45min
Max altitude	On the trail before Mürren at around 1655m
Refreshments	Several options in Gimmelwald, all options in Mürren
Access	Cable car/train from Lauterbrunnen valley

Gimmelwald is a quiet mountain village with a population of around 100, mainly devoted to a few farms and an excellent restaurant and various accommodations. The old buildings are mainly functional, and it feels a complete contrast to the busyness of Mürren. The walk there is a gentle escape from Mürren's already limited hustle and bustle. The route can be finished by returning the same way, by using the cable car or by climbing through the pastures above the village.

From the centre of **Mürren**, take the signed steps down between buildings. The path trends right, crosses a road then meets the road again. Turn left downhill and pass under the cable of the new lift.

After 10min, take a path that branches off to the left. (It's OK to stay on the farm lane, it will rejoin, but it is longer.) The path drops steeply past a house, and then joins the road turning sharply left before a hairpin. Follow

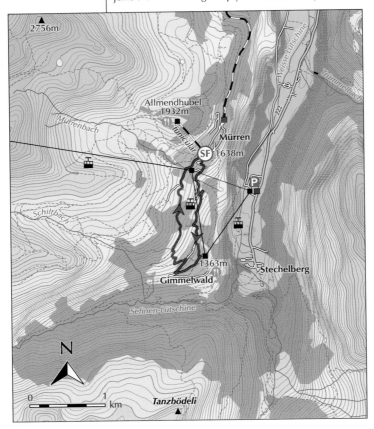

The welcoming Pension Gimmelwald

the road down and at a farm building (Wyleren) take another path left and drop into 'downtown' **Gimmelwald** (1374m, 35min), passing Esther's B&B and coming out at the Pension Gimmelwald (craft beer and Pimms currently available!). ▶

Turn left here for the Schilthornbahn station.

GIMMELWALD

Much quieter than Mürren, Gimmelwald has some fine older buildings and several farms, some of which sell their produce. A trickle of traffic from the cable car has little impact on the tranquillity. It is currently the middle station of the Schilthornbahn between Stechelberg and Mürren, and the redevelopment of the cable car line to go directly from the valley to Mürren will have an impact, although it is promised that the Gimmelwald section will continue to operate for a number of years. When it does finally stop, Gimmelwald is likely to develop an even more 'off the beaten track' feel.

Options from Gimmelwald are to return the way descended in 45–60min. The cable car is always an option. Or follow the route described below.

Walk past Esther's, turn right along the road past houses until coming to a hairpin with fine views into the Sefinental and the Gspaltenhorn at its head. Turn the hairpin and continue up the road. Just after a farm find a sharp left turn on a red and white mountain path. ◄

The path is good, but a bit steeper than those met so far on the walk.

Soon keep left on a farm lane before turning right and steeply up again. Zigzag up the steep meadows where you may see the hay being cut or the carefully manicured fields after clearance. Soon come to a higher lane where there is an option to climb to the Stutz waterfall and Spielbodenalp and its restaurant 300m above (see Walk 42). But turn right along the level track and into woods. Cross a small stream (1535m) after which the path swings left and climbs steeply in the woods in an area called Grabenweidli. There are many routes on this section. Follow the path as it leaves the wood and crosses more pastures and barns. ◄

There are views across to Mürren about 1km away.

The path soon merges with Route 1. Follow this past the lift station and 200 metres more into the centre of **Mürren** (1638, 1hr 45min).

WALK 42
Mürren to the Stutz waterfall and Spielbodenalp

Start/Finish	Mürren 1638m
Distance	7.5km
Total ascent	360m
Total descent	360m
Grade	2
Time	2hr 30min
Max altitude	1797m just above Spielboden
Refreshments	Mürren, Spielbodenalp
Access	Cable car/train from Lauterbrunnen valley

This is a fine walk to the Stutz waterfall in its beautiful setting a little below Spielboden. Much of the route is in the shade of pine woods, with good views when open pastures are crossed. The route can be tackled in either direction, however this is the favoured way as the steep uphill part is in the shade of pine woods, with the superb setting of the waterfall revealed ahead of you. The much easier descent to Mürren in mostly open pasture hillside, where views towards the Eiger can be fully appreciated.

The paths through the woods are steep but well-made, however, care should be taken near the waterfall where some stepped sections are steep and may be loose or slippery. The final part of the route into Mürren is through the 'back door', across a pasture, under the Schilthornbahn and through light woods to emerge in the centre, and is much quieter and prettier than the paved main route.

Leave **Mürren** in the direction of the Schilthorn cable car and continue past the cable car station and up the hill. After 6min take the path to the left signed to Gimmelwald, descend to a chalet and continue right on the path across the front of the chalet (the more distinct path ahead just leads to the chalet below). Enter woodland and begin a steep zigzag descent to **Grabenweidli** (1535m).

Turn right across the stream, and continue almost level for a while, with great views ahead and down to Gimmelwald, to reach a small barn at Bort 2km, 40min. Turn right immediately next to the barn and head steeply up then take the path forking left and enter pine woods. This is a good path that climbs steadily.

After 3km, 1hr 10min the path divides. Take the left path to descend to the **Stutz waterfall**.

The **Schiltbach** creates this lovely waterfall which drops in a series of cascades, some hidden, into a rocky amphitheatre. Higher falls can be seen briefly, then the falls enter into a cleft between rocks, to emerge over an overhanding rock into a fine feathery shoot. Below, the falls have carved a deep narrow gorge.

The narrow cleft through which the Schiltbach flows towards Gimmelwald

Proceed carefully down a steep path with steps, with a cable to grab if needed. Then walk under the water-fall – you will not get wet! Now climb up more steep steps then watch for the path as it turns sharp right signed Bergwanderweg (other paths head downhill).

Climb steeply up through woods to reach a path junction. To the right a path leads more directly to Gimmelwald and Mürren, however, to extend the walk a little continue straight on signed to Spielbodenalp. The path emerges into pastures to shortly arrive at **Spielbodenalp** (1793m, 5km, 1hr 50min, refreshments).

Continue on the path to the right of the restaurant building, descend to cross the Schiltbach stream, then continue on the slightly rising path past a chalet then enter the edge of woods, now descending gently. After 2hr 15min emerge into a meadow, with a path from the waterfall joining from the right. Pass through more woods and meadows to join the main road leading down to Mürren, 2hr 20min.

Descend for just over 100 metres then take a rising path left past a small barn. (If you wish to go directly to Mürren or to the Schilthorn/Stechelberg cable car continue on the road). Climb a little more to an indistinct path junction. ▶ The path to the village continues slightly downhill passing in front of a small barn, under the Schilthorn cable car lines and skirts around the edge of a wooded area. Cross the Mürrenbach stream and continue easily down among chalets, keeping right of Chalet Lora to arrive in the centre of **Mürren** (7.5km, 2hr 30min).

The more obvious steeply rising path to the left leads to an area used by paragliders to launch themselves into the air – well worth a minor detour to watch!

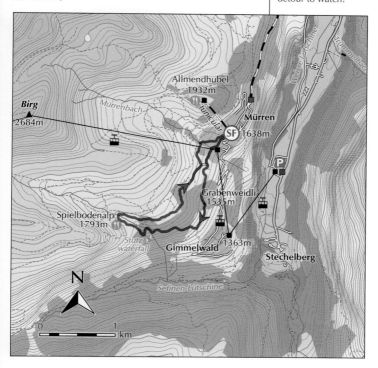

205

WALK 43
Mürren, Bryndli and the Rotstock Hut

Start/Finish	Mürren 1638m
Distance	13.5km
Total ascent	720m
Total descent	720m
Grade	3
Time	5hr
Max altitude	2155m
Refreshments	Mürren, Spielbodenalp, Rotstock hut
Access	Cable car/train from Lauterbrunnen valley

The walk to the Rotstock hut is a popular one, especially on a clear day when the full range of views can be appreciated. The normal direct route follows signs for the Via Alpina, Swiss Route 1, which passes below Bryndli, however this more circular route climbs to the summit with superb views, then along the Wasenegg ridge before a long leisurely descent to the Rotstock hut. The return is entirely on the Via Alpina 1 route.

The route has been graded 3 as there are steep and exposed sections protected by cables on the path up to Bryndli and for the first few minutes along the ridge. These can be avoided if the main Via Alpina route is followed both out and back.

From the centre of **Mürren**, walk south through the village in the direction of the Schilthorn cable car station and continue on the road, climbing steeply through two hairpin bends. Take the signed path on the left after 15min and continue across meadows and through lightly wooded sections to reach **Spielbodenalp** (1791m, 2.4km, 45min, refreshments).

Continue past Spielbodenalp and branch right signed to the Rotstock hut. The path rises gently at first, then soon steepens considerably in tight zigzags up a steep slope sandwiched between rock buttresses. ◄ This is the top of the first steep section of the route 3.5km, 1hr 30min.

Eventually two benches are reached next to an encouraging sign for the Rotstock hut.

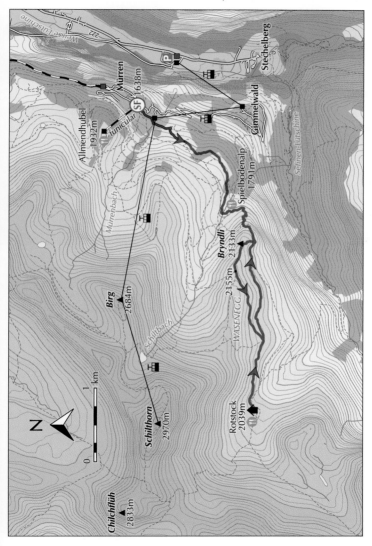

Great views from the summit of Bryndli

Bryndli is a superb vantage point with panoramic views – there is even a summit log book for those wishing to record their ascent.

Continue along the path at a much easier gradient for about 250 metres to reach a sign by two benches pointing to the right for Bryndli. This is a small steep little path with loose soil and stones that tackles the slope in more tight zigzags to reach a sign indicating 'Bryndli 2132m', with the continuing path along the ridge to the left, and a further path to the right up to the actual summit and viewpoint. Take the path to the viewpoint, which is a little exposed at the top, but with a reassuring cable to help. **Bryndli** (2133m, 4km, 1hr 50min). ◄

Return from the viewpoint and turn right to begin the ridge walk. The first section is the most exposed, but the path is well made and there are cables to reassure and protect. Difficulties are soon passed, and a good path rises across a pasture to reach the **high point on this part of the ridge** (2155m). Descend to a path junction immediately ahead and take the descending path angled left, 4.5km, 2hr 20min. Other paths lead further along the ridge, and down into the Schiltalp valley.

The way is now clear for a long and easy descent, with great views ahead towards the Schilthorn (2970m), and the Gspaltenhorn (3436m) over to the left, with the Sefinafurgga the obvious high pass between them. At 2051m after 5.7km the path joins the main Via Alpina 1 path to continue to reach the **Rotstock hut** (2039m, 7km, 3hr, refreshments).

To return to Mürren, retrace the path back climbing a little at first, but then keep to the Via Alpina path which skirts the hillside with minimal height gain or loss. Finally descend with care down the tight zigzags to Spielbodenalp, then continue down to **Mürren** on the same path used for the ascent.

ROTSTOCK HUT 2039M

The Rotstock hut sits in an idyllic situation high among alp pastures at the foot of the long climb to the Sefinafurgga, on the Via Alpina 1 route to Griesalp. It is also on the Rota Hard route to the Schilthorn – a long climb finishing along a shale ridge to the Schilthorn. The hut can accommodate up to 43 overnight, including a private chalet that accommodates two. Food is excellent and it even distils its own gin.

WALK 44
The Sefinental and Rotstock Hut

Start/Finish	Mürren 1638m
Distance	15km
Total ascent	840m
Total descent	840m
Grade	2–3 (3 for the Bryndli descent only)
Time	5hr 15min
Max altitude	2057m
Refreshments	Mürren, Rotstock hut, Spielbodenalp
Access	Cable car/train from Lauterbrunnen valley

The Sefinental is hemmed in between the Schilthorn range, the Gspaltenhorn/Bütlasse mountain wall at its head and the ridge separating the Mürren walks from those of the Upper Lauterbrunnen valley. Although shorter, it is a valley of great beauty and tranquillity, and it would be quite possible to spend a day meandering around its upper reaches. This walk explores the valley and then climbs from the lower Sefinental to the Rotstock hut, which acts as the gateway to the high Sefinafurgga col (see Walk 45) before returning to Mürren on a high traversing path.

Take the Gimmelwald path from the centre of **Mürren**, descending steps and then a farm lane. Take a path left down fields and past a house to rejoin the lane near a hairpin. Follow the lane through **Gimmelwald** (avoiding the signed path unless you need refreshments already). Come to a hairpin at the west end of the village (1393m, 35min).

The beauty and peace of the Sefinental become quickly apparent.

Continue the descent on a track. ◄ Views of the vast rock walls of the Gspaltenhorn and Bütlasse at the head of the valley grow steadily. Pass the turn to Obersteinberg just before **Im Tal** and its peaceful meadows (1258m, 55min).

From here the path becomes wonderful and isolated, with the mountain wall growing steadily in front of you and the **Sefinen-Lütschine** stream racing below. Climb steadily, the track becomes a path, and come to a **junction** at 1418m, 1hr 30min.

To continue to the head of the valley keep left at this junction. There are numerous picnic places at the foot of the **Gspaltenhorn**. Allow 30min each way for the walk, but allow much longer for appreciating the scenery. The mountain wall can be viewed much closer, but not necessarily better as it is foreshortened.

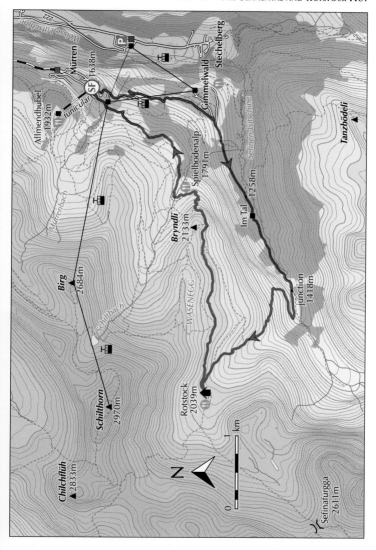

THE GSPALTENHORN

At 3436m, the Gspaltenhorn is not one of the Bernese 4000m giants, but its 1800m north face (which matches the Eiger) suggests this is a significant mountain. The first ascent was by guides J. Anderegg, H. Baumann, with G.E. Foster in 1869. The north face attracted the attention of German climber Willo Welzenbach in 1932, whist the complete north face route was only established in 1951 by Swiss climbers Reiss, Schatz and Haltiner, well after the 1938 Eiger route was climbed.

The trail into the Sefinental with the Gspaltenhorn (on the left) and Bütlasse peaks at its head

The climb to the Rotstock hut starts gently, but soon steepens. With the Gspaltenhorn/Bütlasse wall ahead and the rock spires of the upper Sefinental above, the trail rises in magnificent scenery. The path enters shading woods for a while, but then climbs through more open higher pastures. At 1837m pass a path to the right going to the Oberlager farm, and keep left. The hut and adjacent dairy farm are visible ahead 200m higher and 30min away. The path is clearly waymarked, and joins the Alpina Route 1 shortly before you arrive at the **Rotstock hut** (2039m, 3hr 15min).

THE ROTSTOCK HUT

This SAC hut sits strategically along the Via Alpina route between Mürren and Griesalp at the foot of the climb to the Sefinafurgga as well as the Rota Hard Schilthorn ascent. It has long had a fine culinary reputation and even makes its own gin! The Boganggenalp farm is next door, so a visit to the hut has a background of gently ringing cowbells, but the milk is fresh!

To return to Mürren take the Via Alpina route 1. For 45min the path is almost entirely level, but then descends the steep but not tricky spur of Bryndli, coming out at the inn at **Spielbodenalp** (1791m, 4hr 30min, refreshments).

Continue on Route 1 past the inn, crossing meadows, past farms and barns, above the wood where you can hear deer and partridge and descend steadily into **Mürren** (1638m, 5hr 15min).

WALK 45
Mürren to Griesalp on the Via Alpina

Start	Mürren 1638m
Finish	Griesalp 1408m
Distance	16.5km
Total ascent	1020m
Total descent	1250m
Grade	3
Time	7hr
Max altitude	2611m on the Sefinafurgga
Refreshments	Mürren, Spielbodenalp, then Rotstock hut after 2hr 15min and then only at Golderli Berggasthaus just before Griesalp. Hotel and restaurant in Griesalp
Access	To return to Mürren is a slightly tricky journey via Reichenbach, Spiez and Interlaken then train/bus/lift to Mürren in around 3hr

For those who want to explore outside the valley, this route explores the upper Sefinental, crosses the high and challenging col of the Sefinafurgga and descends to the quiet Kiental and the tiny village at its head, Griesalp. The Sefinafurgga is one of the sternest cols on the Via Alpina/Swiss Route 1 and is best done under good weather conditions. The ascent is steep, and the descent is on wooden steps over shale and should be taken with care.

Combined with Walks 14, 19 and 35 this describes a traverse of the central part of the Bernese Oberland from Meiringen to Griesalp, over 4 days. It could be finished off with another crossing of a high col – the Hohtürli to Kandersteg (see Cicerone's guide to the Swiss Via Alpina).

Note there are many spellings on maps and signs, but we have followed the Swisstopo map and used the spelling Sefinafurgga. However spelled, it's still high and steep.

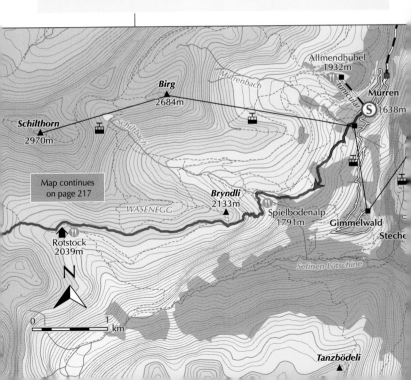

Map continues on page 217

Headed up to the Sefinafurgga

From the centre of **Mürren**, turn south past the Schilthorn cable-car station and after about 400m, when a sign announces a choice of routes to the Sefinafurgga, take the left-hand option signed Route 1. This crosses meadows from which the Breithorn (at the head of the Lauterbrunnental) and Gspaltenhorn (ahead) hold your attention. Pass farms and woods and cross the Schiltbach to come to **Pension Spielbodenalp** (1791m, 50min).

The continuing path now tackles the short but steep Wasenegg spur by a series of zigzags (some exposure), then at the top of the slope, just below the sharp peak of **Bryndli** 2133m, you come to some bench seats (2025m) where the trail forks. Contour round the hillside into a large pastureland where you come to the Oberlager junction (2051m). Continue to the **Rotstock Hut** (2039m, 2hr 15min) seen ahead.

Ahead lies a large basin of rough grass and rocks, on the western side of which the final ascent to the pass begins. The path makes its way over old moraine banks

215

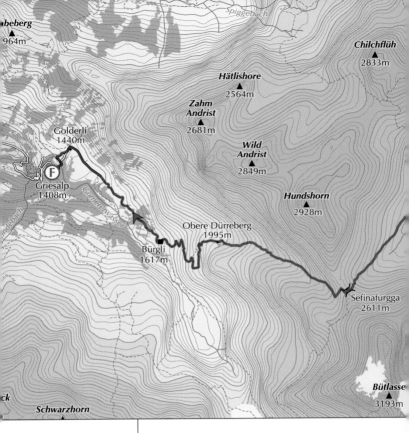

with the Sefinafurgga seen ahead long before you reach it. The last part of the climb ascends a steep zigzag route over slopes of gritty black shale and scree with a short section of wooden steps near the col, to arrive on the **Sefinafurgga** (2611m, 4hr), about 1hr 45min after leaving the Rotstock Hut.

> The **Sefinafurgga** is a narrow, craggy dip in a ridge running from the Hundshorn in the north, to the Bütlassa in the south. (This latter peak is connected to the Gspaltenhorn by a short linking ridge.)

Turning back for a last eastward glance, both Eiger and Mönch, though far off, hold their stature, while in the opposite direction (if you go round the rocks to the left) the glacier-hung Blümlisalp massif signals a major presence only a comparatively short distance ahead to the south-west.

A long line of wooden steps ease the passage over the steep shale after the crossing of the col

The steep descent on the western side of the pass is notable for a seemingly endless stairway of steps, avoiding what had previously been a potentially dangerous slide on unstable slopes of shale and grit. Below the stairway a good path descends yet more shale before grassy hillocks take over, with a small stream breaking through a gully on your left. Following this down, a little over an hour from the pass you come to the small farm building of **Obere Dürreberg** (1995m, 5hr 15min).

Below the farm, cross to the left bank of the stream where the path winds down a steep hillside under the gaze of the Blümlisalp. The alp farms of Untere and Oberi Bundalp can be seen across the valley to the west, appearing small and remote – these will be visited on the next stage of the Via Alpina route to the Hohtürli. On reaching the farm of **Bürgli** (1617m), bear right across the Dürrenberg stream and follow the farm road which leads down to Griesalp in another 35min. Continuing on the main route to Griesalp, shortly after passing Steinenberg come to **Golderli** (1440m, 6hr 45min, refreshments).

The road forks here. Take the left branch and follow this for a few minutes down to **Griesalp** (1408m, 7hr).

GRIESALP (1408M)

This is a tiny hamlet ranged around a square at the end of a narrow toll road that rises through the gentle Kiental valley. Small, specially built postbuses serve the hamlet from Kiental village, on what is said to be Europe's steepest postbus route. With the Tschingelsee below, spectacular high mountain scenery above, accessible neighbouring valleys, and some tough pass crossings to challenge, Griesalp makes a fine base for a walking, climbing or ski-mountaineering holiday away from the bustle of larger Oberland resorts with their international appeal.

For accommodation there's a complex of non-budget hotels: the Berghaus, Grand, Griesschlüchtli, Raspintli and Kurhaus Hohtürli (www.griesalp-hotels.ch). Golderli with rooms and dormitory places is the more economical place to stay, www.golderli.ch.

STECHELBERG AND UPPER
LAUTERBRUNNEN VALLEY

Berghotel Obersteinberg's various buildings all enjoy magnificent views (Walk 48)

WALK 46
Stechelberg – Gimmelwald – Mürren

Start	Stechelberg Schilthornbahn station 862m
Finish	Mürren 1638m
Distance	6.5km
Total ascent	800m
Total descent	25m
Grade	1–2
Time	3hr
Max altitude	Mürren at 1638m
Refreshments	Stechelberg (hotel), Gimmelwald (various) and Mürren (all)
Access	From Mürren take the cable car to the valley terminus and walk from there

This almost entirely uphill walk climbs through the pastoral landscape below Mürren. The facing valley walls on the Jungfrau side feel almost within touching distance, disorientingly close. A gentle valley walk from the bottom of the Schilthornbahn lift to the tranquil head of the valley is followed by a climb on an attractive path alongside the Sefinen Lütschine which drains the Sefinental, before climbing again to picturesque Gimmelwald and likely refreshments, then a final hour on easy farm roads and paths into Mürren.

For those who prefer their walks to be downhill, the route can be **walked in reverse** to Gimmelwald and to Stechelberg with a cable car finish. Allow 1hr 45min to 2hr.

From the cable car exit, go straight across the parking area and cross the bridge over the **Weisse Lütschine** and turn left. After 15min, pass a turn to the hamlet of Stechelberg. Continue ahead, and after a further 10min cross the river on a rounded bridge and pass between electricity

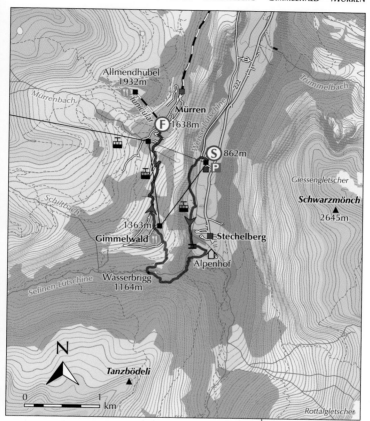

generation buildings to meet a road. Refreshments at the Hotel Stechelberg and transport are to the left.

Turn right passing the **Alpenhof B&B** (30min). The path climbs steeply across a meadow before entering woods. Although steep the path is good. After 30–40min, at a junction called Schwendiwald, meet a path and keep right. Pass two attractive waterfalls, and descend to the bridge at **Wasserbrigg** (1164m, 1hr 15min). ▶

Here there is a choice – either directly up the hillside to Gimmelwald in 35min or a much longer but easier route on tracks, taking an hour.

Mürren sits on the rock walls above Stechelberg

The path now is designated a mountain path, but in fact is very good, just perhaps a bit steeper than before. After a short section of old sunken lane, cross several farm tracks. Keep right at the first after 5min, then left onto a path after a further 5min and then left again 5min later. The meadows are harvested for hay, whilst the buttresses across the valley rise directly above you here. All is signed so keep an eye open for markings. Cross a farm lane near a large building labelled Am Waldrand and climb steadily into **Gimmelwald** (1363m, 2hr).

If needed the cable car station is 2min to the right.

Meet the 'main street' in Gimmelwald by the Pension Gimmelwald. ◄ Take a path headed upwards and to the right above Esther's B&B and follow this until it merges with the farm road at Wyleren where there may be local produce for sale. Keep to the track and 60 metres after a left hairpin, look out for another path angled back sharply to the right. This climbs and soon rejoins the farm lane, passing under the new lift cables. Keep right at a junction and climb steps into the centre of **Mürren** (1638m, 3hr).

For a **finish across high pastures**, see Walk 41 between Gimmelwald and Mürren.

WALK 47

Mürren to Obersteinberg via the Tanzbödeli

Start	Mürren 1638m
Finish	Obersteinberg 1778m
Distance	9km
Total ascent	950m
Total descent	810m
Grade	3
Time	4hr 15min
Max altitude	2133m on the Tanzbödeli
Refreshments	Mürren, Gimmelwald, then no more on the route
Access	See Walks 49 and 50 for onward routes from Obersteinberg. Walk 48 from Stechelberg can be reversed in 2hr 30min for a 7hr-long walking day

The Hinteres Lauterbrunnental – the upper Lauterbrunnen valley – is perhaps the walker's gem of the whole region. Protected as part of the UNESCO world heritage site, as well as a range of local protections and organisations, there has been little or no development and its quiet mystery and mountain inns makes it a place to spend a few days exploring.

This route from Mürren drops down into the quiet Sefinental before climbing steeply to a well-known feature – the Tanzbödeli – a flat meadow on a mountain ridge. This can be avoided if conditions are unsuitable, or you don't fancy the extra stiff climb of 150m. The last section is a high traverse to Obersteinberg with views to the valley below and mountains above the head of the valley.

From the centre of **Mürren** take the stepped path down to Gimmelwald. After the initial twists and turns, take the signed left off the road across pastures, then rejoin the road near a sharp hairpin bend. ▶ Continue along the farm lane through **Gimmelwald** (1393m, 35min) until a hairpin in the road.

From here you get glimpses of the mysteries of the Hinteres Lauterbrunnental, the upper Lauterbrunnen valley.

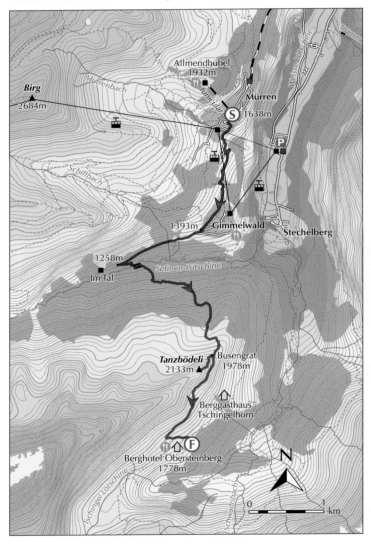

Continue straight ahead at the hairpin now on a track steadily descending into the Sefinental. The mountain wall ahead includes the Gspaltenhorn and the Bütlassa peaks. As you approach **Im Tal**, a pasture and clearing, take the path sharply left at 1258m onto another track, and then continue down turning right then bending left to a bridge across the **Sefinen-Lütschine** (1238m, 1hr).

It's a long climb on a good but steep path in woods for the first 600m of uphill from here on. The path skirts under the rocks seen across the valley, occasionally comes to spots with viewpoints back to Gimmelwald, Mürren and the Lauterbrunnen valley, but is mainly in the forest. At 1772m after 2hr 20min having climbed 530m, come to Busenalp signs which head right into a substantial high pasture. But we continue directly up, the trees thinning now to meet the ridge at **Busengrat** (1978m, 2hr 50min).

The traverse after the Busengrat crossing

Here there is a choice. The path to Tanzbödeli heads right, the traverse to Obersteinberg heads left. The **Tanzbödeli** takes around 45min up and down, plus time spent on the top. ◄ Once there the area is a round 40–50 metre wide platform at about 2200m, level with views in all directions. Whether you make the climb or not probably depends on the weather and your need for refreshments after the climb.

The path is good but steepens towards the top to the extent that hands may be helpful.

To continue to Obersteinberg, head straight on. The path is cut into the steep hillside and well-crafted, although it could be challenging if there is snow lying. ◄ It weaves between ribbons of rock, before making a sharp turn left and dropping down to Obersteinberg. Emerge near some farm buildings and turn right for the **Berghotel Obersteinberg** (1778m, 4hr 15min) or left for the **Berggasthaus Tschingelhorn** in a further 15–20min.

The hotel and the upper valley are visible from about half-way along the traverse.

OBERSTEINBERG AND TSCHINGELHORN

Berghotel Obersteinberg and Berggasthaus Tschingelhorn are 15–20min apart at the trail end. Both are fine traditional mountain hostelries with rooms, dorm places and excellent food, well-positioned for higher routes in the valley (see Walks 49 and 50). Obersteinberg has no electricity or internal water, so dinners are by candlelight, and washing is outside. Both have stunning views of the Breithorn and the 3750–3900m peaks on the vast mountain wall south from the Jungfrau, as well as the substantial Schmadribachfall waterfall.

WALK 48

Stechelberg to Obersteinberg

Start	Hotel Stechelberg 910m
Finish	Hotel Obersteinberg 1778m
Distance	8.5km
Total ascent	890m
Total descent	20m
Grade	2
Time	3hr 15min
Max altitude	1778m
Refreshments	Trachsellauenen, Obersteinberg
Access	By cable car then bus to Stechelberg hotel/Rütti

This is effectively a walk in two halves. Between Stechelberg and Trachsellauenen the path is broad gravel, and shared with plentiful walkers making their way up for refreshments. Beyond Trachsellauenen, the path is both narrower and often steeper, and you will find you are almost entirely on your own – and yet this is by far the most memorable part of the route as you enter this wonderful UNESCO protected area.

Steep flights of stone and log steps are interspersed with brief sections of slightly easier gradient, all the while accompanied by the constant thunderous roar of water as it crashes and spits through countless cascades. The path is mainly under a canopy of mixed woodland, with lush under flora and frequent views, only emerging above the tree line at Obersteinberg.

From the bus stop at **Hotel Stechelberg** walk up the road and take the left fork signed for Obersteinberg and immediately begin to climb on a broad gravel track. After about 20min ignore the first bridge crossing the torrent but cross on the second bridge 2min later. The path rises, crossing straight over another broader track, and continues up through two hairpin bends. Shortly after, fork right from the track onto the signed path, which alternates steep and slightly easier sections to reach **Berggasthaus Trachsellauenen** (1202m, 1hr, refreshments).

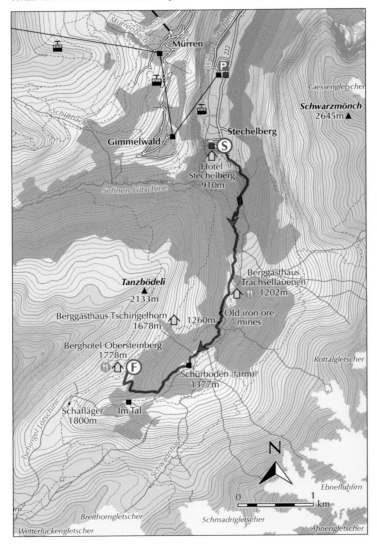

Continue ahead on a track which swings left at a parking area passing the remains of **old iron ore mining buildings** and climb to reach a 'T' junction of paths by a water trough (1260m, 3.3km, 1hr 15min). Both directions are signed to Obersteinberg. ▸

Take the left-hand path which almost immediately climbs steeply with stone steps in tight zigzags up about 100m through a small gorge. At a path junction take the slightly smaller path to the right across a mellow, almost level area of bilberries and juniper to a small group of alp buildings and water trough at **Schürboden** (1377m, 4.9km, 1hr 45min).

Continue, now climbing again, passing a path to the left signed to the Talbach waterfalls, then up more steep steps through another ravine with the constant roar of the water below, to arrive at a small shoulder and path junction.

The path ahead leads to Im Tal (known for being a 'hot spot' – a zone of enhanced energy) then on up a final steep climb to **Schafläger** (1800m), where the final almost level path crosses the stream to the right to Obersteinberg.

The path to the right is signed 1hr 20min and climbs steeply up the hillside to the Berggasthaus Tschingelhorn, then on to Obersteinberg.

Steep steps through lush woodland are a feature for most of this walk

The shorter more direct route now climbs more steep wooden steps at the top of which are superb views of the spectacular Schmadribach waterfall. Continue steeply, then through three broad zigzags now above the tree line to reach the **Hotel Obersteinberg** (1778m, 8.5km, 3hr 15min).

WALK 49
Obersteinberg – Oberhornsee – Stechelberg

Start	Hotel Obersteinberg 1778m
Finish	Hotel Stechelberg 910m
Distance	11km
Total ascent	420m
Total descent	1290m
Grade	2
Time	4hr 30min
Max altitude	Oberhornsee 2065m
Refreshments	Berghotel Obersteinberg, Berggasthaus Tschingelhorn. Trachsellauenen is 20min off route

This stunningly beautiful walk to Oberhornsee takes you high into a huge mountain bowl crowned by the peaks of the Breithorn and Tschingelhorn towering above, whose glaciers still glisten in contrast with the largely snow-free peaks. The climb to the lake takes just over an hour, after which this route makes a circuit passing the viewpoint at the Oberhorn, then descends via a smaller path before rejoining the main path back to Obersteinberg.

From Obersteinberg a good path descends easily to the Berggasthaus Tschingelhorn, another mountain hotel enjoying fine views. The descending route now hugs the hillside descending continuously through woodland, the path full of gnarled tree roots which both prevent slipping (assuming it is dry), but are equally designed to make you trip! The final descent is on a broad gravel path that rejoins the original ascent route of Walk 48.

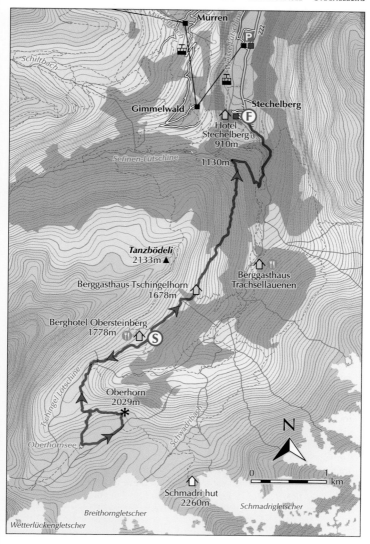

Leave **Hotel Obersteinberg** and head south towards the head of the valley. Views ahead are impressive. The path is mainly fairly level, then drops to cross the Tschingel Lütschine torrent. Take the right-hand path signed for the Oberhornsee and climb steadily at first. Pass a path joining from the left – this will be your descent path from the Oberhorn viewpoint. The main path now climbs steadily to reach the **Oberhornsee** (2.7km, 1hr 10min), a beautiful spot surrounded by glaciers, waterfalls and mountains.

Take the path that initially crosses just to the north of the Oberhornsee, then heads north-east on an almost flat path beside the Chrummbach stream to reach a bridge. ◀

To the right across the bridge leads to the Schmadri Hut (see Walk 50).

Take the left path heading across pasture and past two alp buildings to reach a flat viewpoint area (**Oberhorn**, 2029m) with fine views down the valley and up to the south side of the Jungfrau. The descending narrow path drops immediately and steeply on stone steps, then eases across an area filled with bilberry bushes before dropping again to re-join the main path back to **Obersteinberg** (6.6km, 2hr 40min).

Walking past the hotel and associated farming buildings, continue on the path heading north slightly downhill crossing a ravine and through light woods to reach **Berghaus Tschingelhorn** (1678m, 7.6km, 3hr).

Pass in front of the *Berggasthaus* and take the path ahead (the steep path to the right heads to Trachsellauenen). Crossing steep grassy hillside with juniper and bilberry bushes, the path enters mixed woodland about 30min later. From here on the path is a tangled web of gnarled tree roots, many forming natural steps, but many more designed to keep you focussed on where your feet go with every step. ◀ It's steep all the way, and shouldn't be rushed, but it's also a pretty path and provides good shade from the sun for most of the way. In wet weather the roots will be very slippery and the route best avoided.

Occasional breaks in the trees reveal views across to the Jungfrau, or north as far as Wengen.

Briefly pass just above an open pasture, re-enter woods then drop to meet a wide gravel track at 1130m, 9.5km, 4hr. Turn right and head easily downhill, to join

another track on a bend. Turn left and continue downhill, crossing straight over another track to continue on the gravel path down to **Stechelberg** 4hr 30min.

A walker admires the views from just below the Berggasthaus Tschingelhorn

Summer flowers line the path to the Oberhornsee

WALK 50

Obersteinberg – Oberhornsee –
Schmadri Hut – Stechelberg

Start	Obersteinberg, 1778m
Finish	Stechelberg 910m
Distance	13km
Total ascent	680m
Total descent	1550m
Grade	3
Time	5hr 30min
Max altitude	2260m at the Schmadri Hut
Refreshments	Obersteinberg, then none on the route until Trachsellauenen, Stechelberg at the end of the walk. The Schmadri Hut is unmanned
Access	See Walks 46 and 47 for routes to Obersteinberg. Return to Mürren by the Schilthornbahn lift

This exploration of the higher reaches of the Upper Lauterbrunnen valley is one of our favourite walks in the book. Starting high after an overnight stay in one of the mountain inns, it climbs higher to the beautiful Oberhornsee lake, and after crossing a moraine, climbs to the remote unmanned Schmadri Hut, before beginning a long descent into the lower valley and back to Stechelberg.

The paths are good throughout, the position in amongst the peaks and glaciers is exceptional, whilst the designation of the area as a UNESCO World Heritage site ensures the pristine beauty is preserved and the mountain inns make for a great overnight base. Refreshments are limited until near the end, so take adequate provisions and hope for great weather for this exceptional route.

Head south from **Obersteinberg**, and after 20 metres take the upper path to Oberhorn (a viewpoint) and Oberhornsee, the beautiful glacial lake. The Schmadribachfall is constantly in view, whilst the

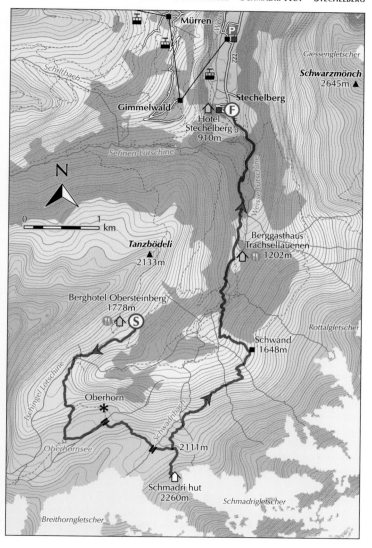

higher peaks and glaciers become steadily clearer as you continue. The path rises very gradually, until dropping to cross the Tschingel Lütschine. From here there are options left to Oberhorn, but take the path right and climb the path to the **Oberhornsee** (2065m, 1hr 10min).

The **lake** is tiny, maybe 30 metres across, but it sits in a bowl with glaciers and mountains in all directions. The Breithorn, Tschingelhorn and Wätterhoren (Lauterbrunnen Wetterhorn) and their glaciers tower above, but the tranquillity of the lake remains. You are unlikely to have it all to yourself, but a path runs round it, so finding quiet rest spots is straightforward. A path heads right towards the Tschingelfirn glacier, the start of a long glacial crossing to the Kanderfirn and Kandersteg.

The beautiful Oberhornsee

Continue past the lake and gradually descend alongside a stream. After 20min meet the Oberhorn path, but here turn right across a bridge and climb a substantial moraine (the Oberhornmoräne) before dropping to another bridge and continuing to a **path junction at 2111m** (2hr 10min).

Glaciers (still) tumble down from the Breithorn and Tschingelhorn

> The round trip to the **Schmadri Hut** is around 45min with 150m of up and down, the hut is unmanned with no services but makes another fine viewpoint over the glaciers of the upper valley.

The climb to the hut is up a well-graded moraine before a final steep pull to the hut. It's interesting to see the facilities in this unmanned hut, a starting point for climbs on the Breithorn but also a fine spot to spend the night, so long as you have brought your own food and sleeping bag. Having feasted on the view, drop down again to the **2111m junction** (2hr 50min).

Turn right and head steadily down. The path takes a long traverse as it descends under the glaciers of the

The Lauterbrunnen Wetterhorn and Tschingelhorn above the Oberhornsee (Walk 50)

Grosshorn and Mittaghorn, before emerging at the long visible farm at **Schwand** (1648m, 4hr). ▶

Descend steeply and directly for 300m towards the valley before heading into woods, all the while continuing down. Meet another path at 1350m, and cross the **Weisse Lütschine**. Now the Schmadri and Tschingel streams have merged, this is a substantial and sometimes furious torrent. Climb a little and descend a long staircase with the river crashing unseen in a gorge below then steadily down alongside the river before taking a left on the path to arrive at the **Berggasthaus Trachsellauenen** (1202m, 4hr 50min) with refreshments, meals and rooms.

Continue along the path which starts above the road, before meeting it a couple of times, sharing with it, and crossing it finally then also crossing the river near houses at Sichellauenen. The path continues down into **Stechelberg** (910m, 5hr 30min) with refreshments at the hotel, information on the valley and buses for onward transport. ▶

Possible cheese for sale and maybe other refreshments, but look out for the goats.

The cable car to Gimmelwald and Mürren is 30min walk away on the right bank of the river if desired.

APPENDIX A
Useful contacts

Local Tourist Offices

Jungfrau region information and transport
tel 033 828 72 33
Jungfrau.ch

Grindelwald
Dorfstrasse 110, 3818 Grindelwald
tel 033 854 12 12
Located in the sports centre near the station.

Wengen
Wengiboden, 3823 Lauterbrunnen
tel 033 856 85 85
Located next to cable car station to Männlichen.

Mürren
Höhematte 1074b, 3825 Mürren
tel 033 856 86 86
Located in the sports centre.

Lauterbrunnen
Stutzli 460, 3822 Lauterbrunnen
tel 033 856 85 68

Stechelberg
tel 033 855 10 32

Interlaken
Marktgasse, Postfach 1, 3800 Interlaken
tel 033 826 53 00

Tourist Information

Switzerland Tourism (UK)
tel 00800 100 200 29 (free)
Email info@myswitzerland.com
www.myswitzerland.com

Swiss National Tourist Office (USA)
tel (212) 757 5944
Email info.usa@myswitzerland.com

Swiss Tourism Australia
tel 0011 800 100 200 30
Email info.aus@myswitzerland.com

Swiss Alpine Club
www.sac.cas.ch

Swiss Hiking Trail Federation
www.schweizmobil.ch

Map suppliers

Stanfords
tel 0207 836 1321
Email sales@stanfords.co.uk
www.stanfords.co.uk

The Map Shop
tel 01684 593146
0800 085 40 80 (UK only)
Email themapshop@btinternet.com
www.themapshop.co.uk

Swisstopo www.swisstopo.admin.ch

USA Omnimap.com

Apps

Meteoswiss – Swiss weather forecasting

SBB Mobile – all Swiss public transport

OUI.sncf – French rail booking

Swiss Map – Swisstopo and Swiss Mobility mapping to buy and download

Phonemaps – open data mapping with footpaths

Outdooractive – mapping and routes.
Open data maps, with options to purchase
Swisstopo maps

Trainline – cross-European rail tickets

Mountain huts and restaurants

The list below highlights the main huts
and restaurants which would allow good
opportunities for splitting or combining
routes.

Faulhorn hut
Located almost at the summit of the
Faulhorn, experience sunsets and
alpenglow on the Eiger, in a truly
magnificent location. A great place
to stay, featured in Walks 2 and 3.
Accommodation in traditional dormitories
plus 6 double, 1 quadruple and 2 family
rooms.
tel 079 534 99 51
www.faulhorn.ch

First Berggasthaus
Ideal for combining a variety of walks;
2, 3, 4, 5, 9 and 10, with superb views,
this is a tranquil spot at night when day
visitors have departed. Accommodation
in refurbished rooms sleeping 2–8 people,
and dormitories.
tel 033 828 77 88
www.berggasthausfirst.ch

Hotel Wetterhorn
Linking Walks 8, 9 and 14, this
friendly hotel offers single, double
and family rooms as well as dormitory
accommodation.
tel 033 853 12 18
www.wetterhorn-hotel.ch

Grosse Scheidegg Berghotel
The roadside location provides good
opportunities to combine walks with
postbus transport, and the opportunity to
link walks on both sides of the pass. Various
options in simple rooms and dormitories.
tel 033 853 67 16
www.grosse-scheidegg.ch/

Alpiglen Berghaus
Spectacular location at the foot of the
Eiger, just below the Eiger Trail. Useful for
linking various walks including 19, 20, 21
and 22. Accommodation in double rooms
and 10-bed dormitories.
tel 033 853 11 30
www.alpiglen.ch

Kleine Scheidegg Berghaus Grindelwaldblick
Sleep below the Eiger, Mönch and
Jungfrau, and be on the trail before tourists
arrive by train. A great location for linking
Walks 19, 20, 21, 23, 29 and 30 and
routes to and around Wengen. Dormitory
accommodation for 66 persons, plus 2 x
double rooms and 1 x 4-bed room.
tel 033 855 13 74
www.grindelwaldblick.ch

Männlichen Berghaus
Ideal for Walks 22, 23 and 27, Männlichen
is easily reached by cable car and
lifts from Wengen and Grindelwald.
Accommodation is mainly double rooms
plus two family rooms. Open June to
October.
tel 033 853 10 68
www.berghaus-maennlichen.ch

Rotstock hut
High above Mürren occupying a grassy
bowl with superb views. Dormitory
accommodation. Open from June to late
September.
tel 033 855 24 64
www.rotstockhuette.ch

Schilthorn hut

A special place to stay with superb views at 2432m. Single dormitory for 25 people in the roof space. Open June to September.
tel 033 855 50 53
www.schilthornhuette.com

Lobhorn Hut

Shared accommodation in a dramatic mountain location with superb views. Easily accessed from Sulwald in 1hr 15min (Walk 32) or from Saxeten (Walk 31), it makes a popular destination, especially at weekends and overnights awaken to stunning views.
tel 079 656 53 20
www.lobhornhuette.ch

Further huts and restaurants

Schynige Platte
tel 033 828 73 73
www.hotelschynigeplatte.ch

Berghaus Männdlenen
tel 033 853 44 64
www.berghaus-maenndlenen.ch

Berggasthaus First
tel 033 828 77 88
www.berggasthausfirst.ch

Schreckfeld Restaurant
tel 033 853 54 30
www.restaurant-schreckfeld.ch/

Bort Alpinhotel
tel 033 853 17 62

Waldspitz Berggasthaus
tel 033 853 18 61
www.gasthaus-waldspitz.ch

Bussalp Restaurant
tel 033 853 37 51

Gleckstein Hut
tel 033 853 11 40

Pfingstegg restaurant
tel 033 853 11 91

Gasthaus Gletscherschlucht
tel 033 853 60 50
www.gletscherschlucht.ch

Marmorbruch
tel 079 310 30 89
www.marmorbruch.ch

Bäregg Berghaus
tel 079 121 09 09
www.baeregg.com

Schreckhorn hut
tel 033 855 10 25

Brandegg Bergrestaurant
tel 033 853 10 57

Kleine Scheidegg Lodge Bergrestaurant
tel 033 828 78 88
www.bergrestaurant-kleine-scheidegg.ch

Kleine Scheidegg Hotel Bellevue des Alpes
tel 033 855 12 12
www.scheidegg-hotels.ch

Grindelwaldblick
tel 033 855 13 74
www.grindelwaldblick.ch

Eigergletscher Schreinerei restaurant
tel 033 828 78 88

Hotel Jungfrau Wengernalp
tel 033 855 16 22
www.wengernalp.ch

Allmend Bergrestaurant
tel 033 855 45 45

Spielboden restaurant
tel 079 646 91 16

Schiltalp restaurant
tel 033 855 13 20

Suppenalp restaurant and pension
tel 033 855 17 26
www.suppenalp.ch

Berghaus Sonnenberg
tel 033 855 11 27
www.restaurant-sonnenberg.ch

Allmendhubel restaurant
tel 033 826 00 07

Winteregg restaurant
tel 033 828 70 90

Sulwald Stubli restaurant
tel 033 855 12 51

Alpenhof Stechelberg
tel 033 855 12 02
www.alpenhof-stechelberg.ch

Berggasthaus Trachsellauenen
tel 033 855 12 35

Berggasthaus Tschingelhorn
tel 033 855 13 43
www.tschingelhorn.ch

Berghaus Obersteinberg
tel 033 855 20 33

Camping

Grindelwald
Camping Gletscherdorf
tel 033 853 14 29
www.gletscherdorf.ch

Camping Eigernordwald
tel 033 853 12 42
www.eigernordwand.ch

Camping Holdrio
tel 079 614 02 88
www.camping-grindelwald.ch

Lütschental
Dany's camping
tel 033 853 18 24
www.danys-camping.ch

Lauterbrunnen
Camping Jungfrau
tel 033 856 20 10
www.campingjungfrau.swiss

Camping Breithorn
tel 033 855 12 25
www.campingbreithorn.ch

Camping Rütti Stechelberg
tel 033 855 28 85
www.campingruetti.ch

Specialist Mountain Activities Insurers

BMC Travel & Activity Insurance
(BMC members only)
tel 0161 445 6111
www.thebmc.co.uk

Austrian Alpine Club
tel 01929 556 870
www.aacuk.org.uk
(AAC membership carries accident and
mountain rescue insurance, plus reciprocal
rights reductions in SAC huts.)

Snowcard Insurance Services
www.snowcard.co.uk

Harrison Beaumont
Pond Hall, Hadleigh, Ipswich IP7 5PP
tel 0345 450 8547
www.hbinsurance.co.uk

APPENDIX B

Trains, lifts, buses and discount options

Trains

- Interlaken West, Interlaken Ost, Wilderswil, Zweilütschinen, Grindelwald Terminal, Grindelwald; Grindelwald Grund to Kleine Scheidegg; and to Lauterbrunnen, Wengen, Kleine Scheidegg, with onward trains to Eigergletscher.

- Train services start at around 6am, through to around 11pm.

- Eigergletscher to Jungfraujoch 08:30, last descent 16:45 (discounted fares, or included with Top of Europe Pass).

- Train from Wilderswil to Schynige Platte. Trains from 07:30, last return 17:50.

- For Mürren, the funicular from Lauterbrunnen to Grütschalp from 6am, then train to Mürren.

Lifts

- Grindelwald to First, from 09:00, final descent 17:30, high season (July to 21 August) 08:00 to 18:00.

- Grindelwald Terminal to Eigergletscher from 08:00, last return 17:10.

- Grindelwald Terminal to Männlichen from 08:45 (08:15 July to mid-August), last return 17:30.

- Wengen to Männlichen 08:50 (08:10 July to mid-August), last descent 17:30.

- Interlaken to Harder Kulm 09:10, last descent 21:40.

- Lake Ferries are also included in the Jungfrau Travel Pass.

- Mürren is served with additional lifts (not included in the Jungfrau pass); Stechelberg – Gimmelwald – Mürren – Berg – Schilthorn 07:25 to 16:25, last descent from Schilthorn 17:55, also Funicular to Allmendhubel 09:00 to 17:00.

- The Jungfrau Travel Pass covers free and unlimited use of these transport systems (for 3–8 days), and a discounted rate for the Eigergletscher to Jungfraujoch train. Other passes and discount cards are available. For more information on passes see the section in the Introduction and the table below.

Buses

Grindelwald

- Good frequent bus services to all parts of Grindelwald are included free for holders of a Guest Card. For details see www.grindelwaldbus.ch. Services include 121 service between Ober Gletscher (Hotel Wetterhorn) to Terminal, 122 between Gletscherschlucht and Klusi via Stutz, and 123 between Kirche and Egg via Terminal.

- Discount cards can be used for reduced fares on the following services: 128 service from Grindelwald to Hotel Wetterhorn and Grosse Scheidegg, and from Grosse Scheidegg to Schwarzwaldalp, and 164 service on to Meiringen. Mountain bus 126 to Bussalp, and Mountain bus 127 to Waldspitz. Also to Interlaken and other destinations from the bus station area next to the main train station.

DISCOUNTS

Card/Pass	Validity	CHF	Train	Bus	Boat	Cities	Museums	Comments
Half Fare Card	1 month	100	X	X	X	X	X	Mountain excursions*
Swiss Travel Pass	Fixed consecutive 3, 4, 6, 8, 15 days	195–358	X	X	X	X	X	Includes lift from valley to Mürren**
Swiss Travel Flex Pass	Flexible 3, 4, 6, 8, 15 days***	225–375	X	X	X	X	X	Includes lift from valley to Mürren**
Regional Pass – Bernese Oberland****	3, 4, 6, 8, 10 days	195–335	X	X	X			Includes lifts, mountain railways, excludes Schilthorn.
Top of Europe	3–8 days	200–285	X					Includes lifts, mountain railways, excludes Schilthorn, Includes one trip to Jungfraujoch
Jungfrau Travel Pass	3–8 days	190 –310						Includes lifts, mountain railways, lake ferries, and discount for Jungfraujoch

* Mountain excursions are Bernina, Glacier and Luzem to Interlaken Express itineraries, and Golden Pass Panoramic.

** Free from valley to Mürren, then ½ price to Schilthorn, and ½ price on mountain railways and lifts, 25% Jungfraujoch, plus discounts on SNCF Lyria trains between France and Switzerland.

*** Book and amend on activateyourpass.com.

**** Free and discounted fares in region – Bern – Luzem – Brig, and ½ fare Montreux to Gstaad.

Note: Subject to change – check carefully when booking.

APPENDIX C
Further reading

General tourist guides

The Rough Guide to Switzerland (Rough Guides, 5th edition 2017)

Switzerland (Lonely Planet, 9th edition 2018)

Essential Switzerland (Fodor's, 1st edition 2018)

Mountains and mountaineering

Recently published or updated books containing references of particular interest to visitors to the Bernese Alps are listed below, as well as classics still in print.

Wanderings Among the High Alps by Sir Alfred Wills (Richard Bentley, London) (Kindle, hardback and paperback).

The Playground of Europe by Leslie Stephen (Longman) (Kindle, hardback and paperback) – Leslie Stephen made a number of first ascents in the Bernese Alps.

The White Spider by Heinrich Harrer (Granada, London. Latest edition published 2005) – Harrer was part of the group that made the first ascent of the Eiger's North Face in 1938. This book recounts the history of attempts on the face up to and including that first ascent.

Eiger Direct by Peter Gillman and Dougal Haston (Vertebrate) (Kindle and paperback)

Alps 4000 by Martin Moran (David & Charles, Devon. 1994) – The account of Moran's and Simon Jenkins's epic journey across all the 4000m summits of the Alps in one summer.

The Alps: High Mountains in Motion by Lorenz Andreas Fischer (teNeues Media GmbH & Co. KG; 1st edition (29 May 2020)) – A stunning photography book of the Alps.

Alpenglow – The Finest Climbs on the 4000m Peaks of the Alps by Ben Tibbetts (1st edition 2019) – An impressive and inspiring book of routes, historic content and photography of the highest Alpine peaks all climbed by the author.

The Swiss Alps by Kev Reynolds (Cicerone Press, 2012) – Describes classic routes for walkers, trekkers, climbers and skiers.

Bernese Oberland: selected climbs by Les Swindin (Alpine Club, London. 2003) – All the major routes, including climbs on the Salbitschijen.

Walking

Trekking the Swiss Via Alpina by Kev Reynolds and Jonathan Williams (Cicerone Press, 4th Edition 2023) – A classic trek that crosses Switzerland and passes through the region.

Walking in the Alps by Kev Reynolds (Cicerone Press, 2nd edition 2010) – Describes walking prospects throughout the Alps, from the Maritime Alps to the Julians of Slovenia.

100 Hut Walks in the Alps by Kev Reynolds (Cicerone Press, 3rd edition 2014) – Includes several huts in the region.

Tour of the Jungfrau Region by Kev Reynolds (Cicerone Press, 3rd edition 2018) – A 9-day trek in the Grindelwald/Mürren district.

Trekking in the Alps by Kev Reynolds (Cicerone Press, 2011) – Among the 20 classic alpine treks described, the Via Alpina and Tour of the Jungfrau Region both feature.

Mountain flowers

Alpine Flowers by Gillian Price (Cicerone Press, 2014) – An excellent and beautifully illustrated pocket guide to 230 alpine flowers.

APPENDIX D
English–German terms

English	German
accident	Unfall
accommodation	Unterkunft
saddle, pass	Sattel
alp	Alp
alpine club	Alpenverein
alpine flower	Alpenblume
avalanche	Lawine
B&B	Hotel garni
bakery	Bäckerei
bedroom	Schlafzimmer
bridge	Brücke
cable car	Drahtseilbahn/Seilbahn
cairn	Steinman
campsite	Zeltplatz
castle	Schloss
chairlift	Sesselbahn
chamois	Gemse
chapel	Kapelle
church	Kirche
combe, small valley	Klumme
common room	Gaststube
crampons	Steigeisen
crest, ridge	Kamm
crevasse	Gletscherspalte

English	German
crevasse between glacier and rock wall	Bergschrund
dangerous	gefährlich
dormitory, simple accommodation	Matratzenlager/Massenlager/Touristenlager
east	Ost
easy	leicht
fog, low cloud, mist	Nebel
spring	Quelle
footpath	Fussweg/Wanderweg
forest	Wald
glacier	Gletscher
gondola lift	Gondelbahn
gorge	Schlucht
greetings	Grüetzi
grocery	Lebensmittel
inn/guest house	Gasthaus/Gasthof
hillwalker	Bergwanderer
holiday apartment	Ferienwohnung
hour(s)	Stunde(n)
ice axe	Pickel
information	Auskunft
lake, tarn	See
landscape	Landschaft
left (direction)	links

English	German
map	Karte
map sheet	Blatt
marmot	Murmeltier
moraine	Moräne
mountain	Berg
mountain guide	Bergführer
mountain hut	Alphütte
mountain inn	Berggasthaus
mountain path	Bergweg
mountaineer	Bergsteiger
roe deer	Reh
north	Nord
pass	Bergpass/Pass
pasture	Weide
path	Pfad
railway station	Bahnhof
ravine	Klamm
reservoir	Stausee
ridge	Grat
right (direction)	rechts
rock wall	Fels
room	zimmer

English	German
rope	Seil
rucksack	Rucksack
scree	Geröllhalde
simple hotel	Pension
slope	Abhang
snow	Schnee
south	Süd
stonefall	Steinschlag
stream, river	Bach
summit, peak	Gipfel
torrent	Wildbach
tourist office	Verkehrsverein
upper	ober
vacancies	Zimmer frei
valley	Tal
via, or over	über
viewpoint	Aussichtspunkt
village	Dorf
water	Wasser
west	West
wooded ravine	Tobel
youth hostel	Jugendherberge

Looking up-valley from the bottom of the trail in Lauterbrunnen (Walk 35)

DOWNLOAD THE ROUTES
IN GPX FORMAT

All the routes in this guide are available for download from:

www.cicerone.co.uk/1114/GPX

as standard format GPX files. You should be able to load them into most online GPX systems and mobile devices, whether GPS or smartphone. You may need to convert the file into your preferred format using a conversion programme such as gpsvisualizer.com or one of the many other such websites and programmes.

When you follow this link, you will be asked for your email address and where you purchased the guidebook, and have the option to subscribe to the Cicerone e-newsletter.

www.cicerone.co.uk

LISTING OF CICERONE GUIDES

Mountain Biking on the
North Downs
Mountain Biking on the
South Downs
Short Walks in the Surrey Hills
Suffolk Coast and Heath Walks
The Cotswold Way
The Cotswold Way Map Booklet
The Kennet and Avon Canal
The Lea Valley Walk
The North Downs Way
The North Downs Way Map Booklet
The Peddars Way and Norfolk
Coast Path
The Pilgrims' Way
The Ridgeway National Trail
The Ridgeway Map Booklet
The South Downs Way
The South Downs Way Map Booklet
The Thames Path
The Thames Path Map Booklet
The Two Moors Way
The Two Moors Way Map Booklet
Walking Hampshire's Test Way
Walking in Cornwall
Walking in Essex
Walking in Kent
Walking in London
Walking in Norfolk
Walking in the Chilterns
Walking in the Cotswolds
Walking in the Isles of Scilly
Walking in the New Forest
Walking in the North Wessex Downs
Walking on Guernsey
Walking on Jersey
Walking on the Isle of Wight
Walking the Jurassic Coast
Walking the South West Coast Path
Walking the South West Coast Path
Map Booklets:
Vol 1: Minehead to St Ives
Vol 2: St Ives to Plymouth
Vol 3: Plymouth to Poole
Walks in the South Downs
National Park

WALES AND WELSH BORDERS

Cycle Touring in Wales
Cycling Lon Las Cymru
Glyndwr's Way
Great Mountain Days in Snowdonia
Hillwalking in Shropshire
Hillwalking in Wales – Vols 1&2
Mountain Walking in Snowdonia
Offa's Dyke Path
Offa's Dyke Map Booklet
Ridges of Snowdonia
Scrambles in Snowdonia
Snowdonia: 30 Low-level and Easy
Walks – North
Snowdonia: 30 Low-level and Easy
Walks – South

The Cambrian Way
The Pembrokeshire Coast Path
The Pembrokeshire Coast Path
Map Booklet
The Severn Way
The Snowdonia Way
The Wye Valley Walk
Walking in Carmarthenshire
Walking in Pembrokeshire
Walking in the Brecon Beacons
Walking in the Forest of Dean
Walking in the Wye Valley
Walking on Gower
Walking the Shropshire Way
Walking the Wales Coast Path

INTERNATIONAL CHALLENGES, COLLECTIONS AND ACTIVITIES

Europe's High Points
Walking the Via Francigena Pilgrim
Route – Part 1

AFRICA

Kilimanjaro
Walks and Scrambles in the
Moroccan Anti-Atlas
Walking in the Drakensberg

ALPS CROSS-BORDER ROUTES

100 Hut Walks in the Alps
Alpine Ski Mountaineering
Vol 1 – Western Alps
Vol 2 – Central and Eastern Alps
The Karnischer Hohenweg
The Tour of the Bernina
Trail Running – Chamonix and the
Mont Blanc region
Trekking Chamonix to Zermatt
Trekking in the Alps
Trekking in the Silvretta and
Ratikon Alps
Trekking Munich to Venice
Trekking the Tour of Mont Blanc
Walking in the Alps

PYRENEES AND FRANCE/SPAIN CROSS-BORDER ROUTES

Shorter Treks in the Pyrenees
The GR10 Trail
The GR11 Trail
The Pyrenean Haute Route
The Pyrenees
Walks and Climbs in the Pyrenees

AUSTRIA

Innsbruck Mountain Adventures
Trekking in Austria's Hohe Tauern
Trekking in Austria's Zillertal Alps
Trekking in the Stubai Alps
Walking in Austria
Walking in the Salzkammergut:
the Austrian Lake District

EASTERN EUROPE

The Danube Cycleway Vol 2
The Elbe Cycle Route
The High Tatras
The Mountains of Romania
Walking in Bulgaria's National Parks
Walking in Hungary

FRANCE, BELGIUM AND LUXEMBOURG

Camino de Santiago – Via Podiensis
Chamonix Mountain Adventures
Cycle Touring in France
Cycling London to Paris
Cycling the Canal de la Garonne
Cycling the Canal du Midi
Cycling the Route des Grandes Alpes
Mont Blanc Walks
Mountain Adventures in the
Maurienne
Short Treks on Corsica
The GR5 Trail
The GR5 Trail – Benelux and
Lorraine
The GR5 Trail – Vosges and Jura
The Grand Traverse of the
Massif Central
The Moselle Cycle Route
The River Loire Cycle Route
The River Rhone Cycle Route
Trekking in the Vanoise
Trekking the Cathar Way
Trekking the GR20 Corsica
Trekking the Robert Louis
Stevenson Trail
Via Ferratas of the French Alps
Walking in Provence – East
Walking in Provence – West
Walking in the Ardennes
Walking in the Auvergne
Walking in the Brianconnais
Walking in the Dordogne
Walking in the Haute Savoie: North
Walking in the Haute Savoie: South
Walking on Corsica
Walking the Brittany Coast Path

GERMANY

Hiking and Cycling in the
Black Forest
The Danube Cycleway Vol 1
The Rhine Cycle Route
The Westweg
Walking in the Bavarian Alps

IRELAND

The Wild Atlantic Way and
Western Ireland
Walking the Wicklow Way

ITALY

Alta Via 1 – Trekking in the Dolomites
Alta Via 2 – Trekking in the Dolomites
Italy's Sibillini National Park
Shorter Walks in the Dolomites
Ski Touring and Snowshoeing in the Dolomites
The Way of St Francis
Trekking in the Apennines
Trekking the Giants' Trail: Alta Via 1 through the Italian Pennine Alps
Via Ferratas of the Italian Dolomites Vols 1&2
Walking and Trekking in the Gran Paradiso
Walking in Abruzzo
Walking in Italy's Cinque Terre
Walking in Italy's Stelvio National Park
Walking in Sicily
Walking in the Aosta Valley
Walking in the Dolomites
Walking in Tuscany
Walking in Umbria
Walking Lake Como and Maggiore
Walking Lake Garda and Iseo
Walking on the Amalfi Coast
Walking the Via Francigena Pilgrim Route – Part 2 Pilgrim Route – Part 3
Walks and Treks in the Maritime Alps

MEDITERRANEAN

The High Mountains of Crete
Trekking in Greece
Walking and Trekking in Zagori
Walking and Trekking on Corfu
Walking in Cyprus
Walking on Malta
Walking on the Greek Islands – the Cyclades

NEW ZEALAND AND AUSTRALIA

Hiking the Overland Track

NORTH AMERICA

Hiking and Cycling the California Missions Trail
The John Muir Trail
The Pacific Crest Trail

SOUTH AMERICA

Aconcagua and the Southern Andes
Hiking and Biking Peru's Inca Trails
Torres del Paine

SCANDINAVIA, ICELAND AND GREENLAND

Hiking in Norway – South
Trekking in Greenland – The Arctic Circle Trail
Trekking the Kungsleden
Walking and Trekking in Iceland

SLOVENIA, CROATIA, SERBIA, MONTENEGRO AND ALBANIA

Mountain Biking in Slovenia
The Islands of Croatia
The Julian Alps of Slovenia
The Mountains of Montenegro
The Peaks of the Balkans Trail
The Slovene Mountain Trail
Walking in Slovenia: The Karavanke
Walks and Treks in Croatia

SPAIN AND PORTUGAL

Camino de Santiago: Camino Frances
Coastal Walks in Andalucia
Costa Blanca Mountain Adventures
Cycling the Camino de Santiago
Cycling the Ruta Via de la Plata
Mountain Walking in Mallorca
Mountain Walking in Southern Catalunya
Portugal's Rota Vicentina
Spain's Sendero Historico: The GR1
The Andalucian Coast to Coast Walk
The Camino del Norte and Camino Primitivo
The Camino Ingles and Ruta do Mar
The Camino Portugues
The Mountains of Nerja
The Mountains of Ronda and Grazalema
The Sierras of Extremadura
Trekking in Mallorca
Trekking in the Canary Islands
Trekking the GR7 in Andalucia
Walking and Trekking in the Sierra Nevada
Walking in Andalucia
Walking in Catalunya – Barcelona
Walking in Portugal
Walking in the Algarve
Walking on Gran Canaria
Walking on La Gomera and El Hierro
Walking on La Palma
Walking on Lanzarote and Fuerteventura
Walking on Madeira
Walking on Tenerife
Walking on the Azores
Walking on the Costa Blanca
Walking the Camino dos Faros

SWITZERLAND

Switzerland's Jura Crest Trail
The Swiss Alps
Tour of the Jungfrau Region
Walking in the Bernese Oberland
Walking in the Engadine – Switzerland
Walking in the Valais
Walking in Ticino
Walking in Zermatt and Saas-Fee

CHINA, JAPAN AND ASIA

Hiking and Trekking in the Japan Alps and Mount Fuji
Hiking in Hong Kong
Japan's Kumano Kodo Pilgrimage
Trekking in Tajikistan

HIMALAYA

Annapurna
Everest: A Trekker's Guide
Trekking in Bhutan
Trekking in Ladakh
Trekking in the Himalaya

MOUNTAIN LITERATURE

8000 metres
A Walk in the Clouds
Abode of the Gods
Fifty Years of Adventure
The Pennine Way – the Path, the People, the Journey
Unjustifiable Risk?

TECHNIQUES

Fastpacking
Geocaching in the UK
Map and Compass
Outdoor Photography
Polar Exploration
The Mountain Hut Book

MINI GUIDES

Alpine Flowers
Navigation
Pocket First Aid and Wilderness Medicine
Snow

For full information on all our guides, books and eBooks, visit our website:
www.cicerone.co.uk

CICERONE

Trust Cicerone to guide your next adventure, wherever it may be around the world...

Discover guides for hiking, mountain walking, backpacking, trekking, trail running, cycling and mountain biking, ski touring, climbing and scrambling in Britain, Europe and worldwide.

Connect with Cicerone online and find inspiration.

- buy books and ebooks
- articles, advice and trip reports
- podcasts and live events
- GPX files and updates
- regular newsletter

cicerone.co.uk